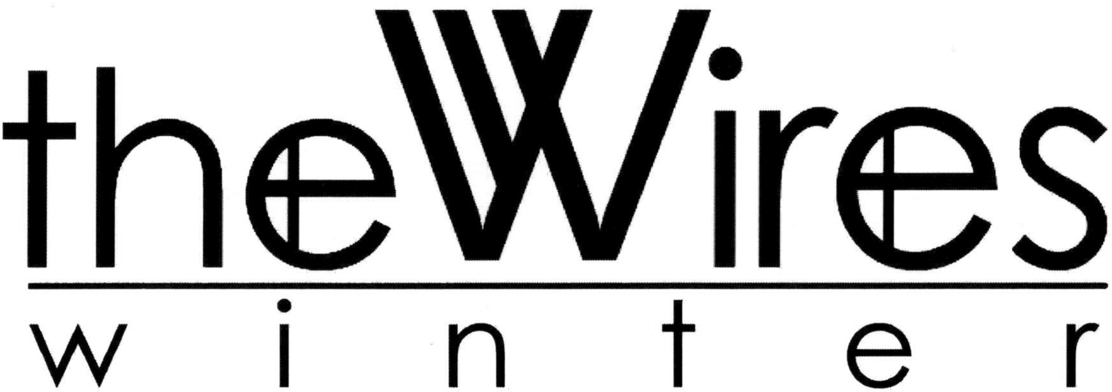


# Folk Carols for Violin and Cello

Laurel Parks and Sascha Groschang

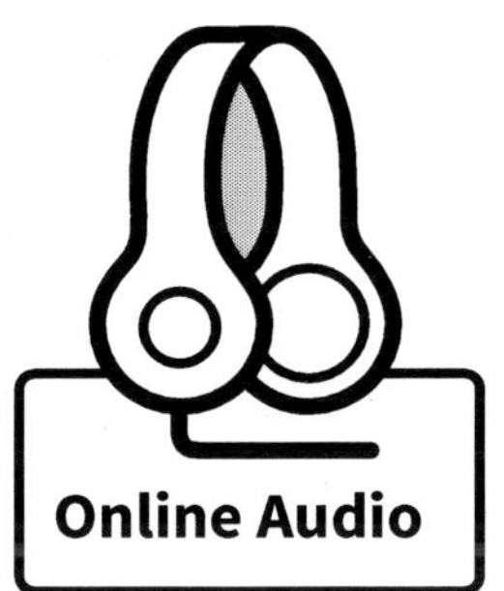


**To access the online audio recording by The Wires Duo go to:**
***WWW.MELBAY.COM/31037MEB***

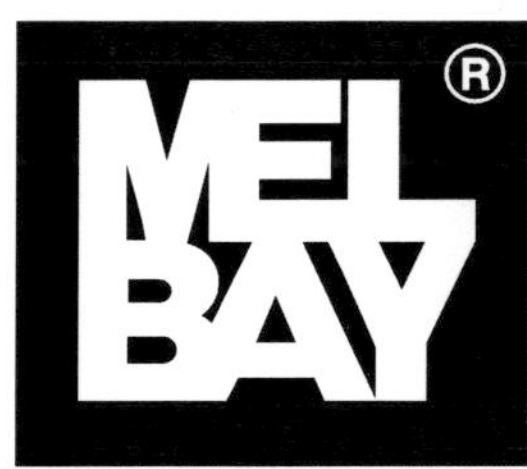



*WWW.MELBAY.COM*

# *Contents*


| Title | Page | Audio |
|---|---|---|
| Lo, How a Rose E're Blooming – Michael Praetorius | 4 | 1 |
| Coventry Carol – Traditional | 6 | 2 |
| Silent Night – Franz Xaver Gruber | 12 | 3 |
| Greensleeves – Traditional | 18 | 4 |
| The Holly and the Ivy – Traditional | 24 | 5 |
| Wexford Carol – Traditional | 28 | 6 |
| Bring a Torch Jeannette, Isabella – Traditional | 32 | 7 |
| In the Bleak Midwinter – Gustav Holst | 36 | 8 |
| Campbell Street – The Wires | 40 | 9 |
| Once in Royal David's City – Henry John Gauntlett | 46 | 10 |
| We Wish You a Merry Christmas – Traditional | 48 | 11 |
| About the Authors | 53 | |

# *Performance Notes*

We've notated many of the ornaments heard on our studio recording "Winter." However, all of these pieces are inspired by folk idioms. Feel free to take away or add your own ornaments, slides and double stops. This music is less rigid than traditional classical music so there is plenty of room for micro-improvisations. In other words, make these pieces your own!

A few specific techniques are used in the cello parts. Several of the tunes use the chopping technique. This technique is indicated by an 'X' notehead. *Greensleeves* and *We Wish You a Merry Christmas* use a strumming pizzicato technique and *We Wish You a Merry Christmas* uses a fingerboard slap, as indicated with a slash notehead.

The chop utilizes a straight thumb and is a combination of dropping the bow heavily on the string and allowing the bow to scrape the strings. Your bow hair will be angled slightly towards the floor, and your contact point will be closer to the bridge than usual. The note after the chop will be a quasi-chop. The act of releasing the bow off the string will create a sort of ghost note, a little bit of pitch will be heard, and a small chopping scrape sound will also be audible.

For the strumming technique, you will use your thumb to pizzicato on the lower strings, away from your body. For the top strings, you will use your 3rd finger to pluck toward your body. For the slap pizzicato technique, you'll slap your fingerboard, allowing the strings to hit the wood to create a nice percussive sound. For each of these techniques, the most important thing is that the groove stays steady, so don't worry too much about perfection!

For video instructions on all 3 techniques: Find "TheWiresDuo" channel on Youtube and search for the "Special Cello Techniques" video: https://www.youtube.com/watch?v=oc34FkDRI_U

# Lo, How a Rose E'er Blooming

1

Michael Praetorius
Arranged by The Wires: Sascha Groschang and Laurel Parks

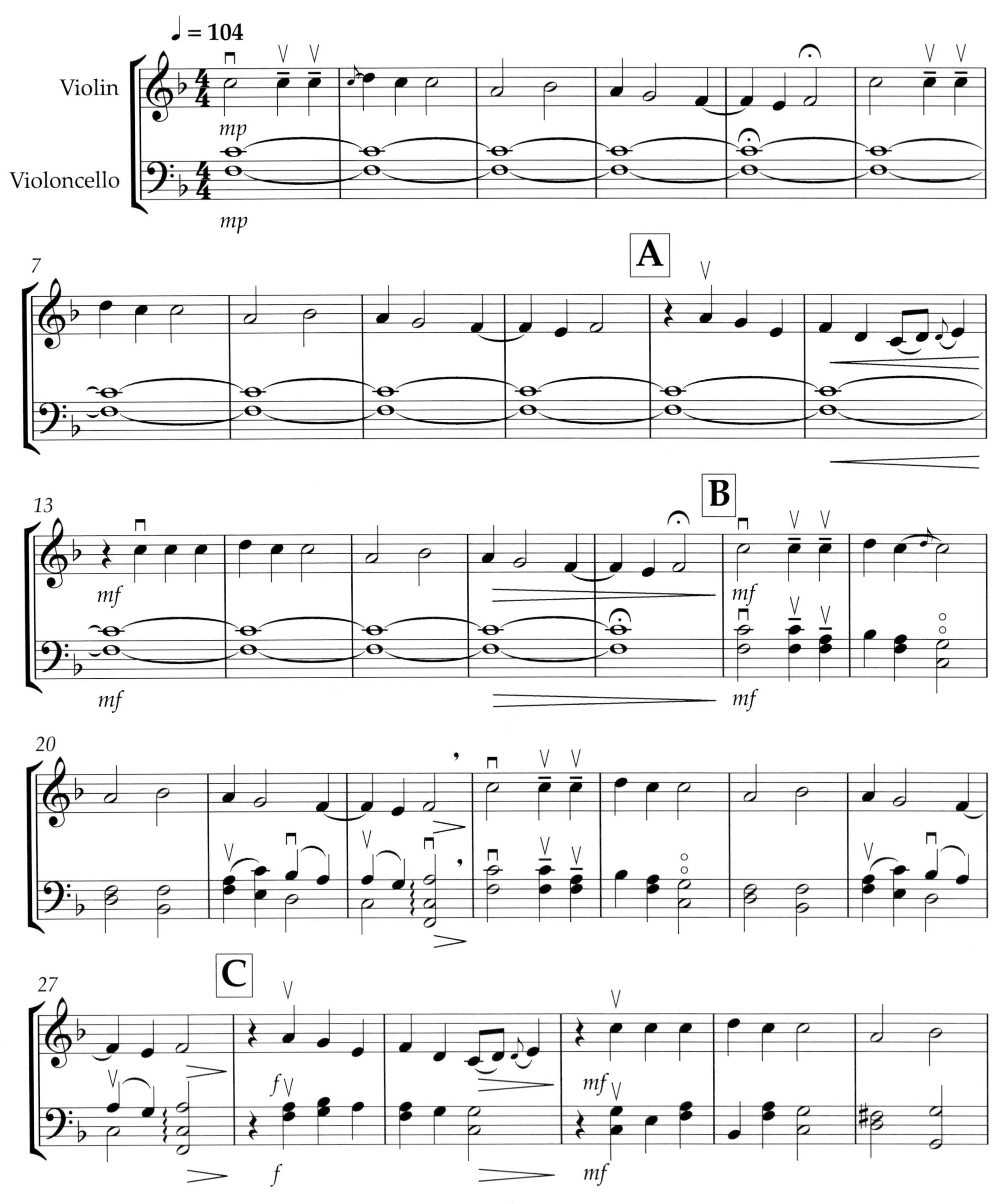

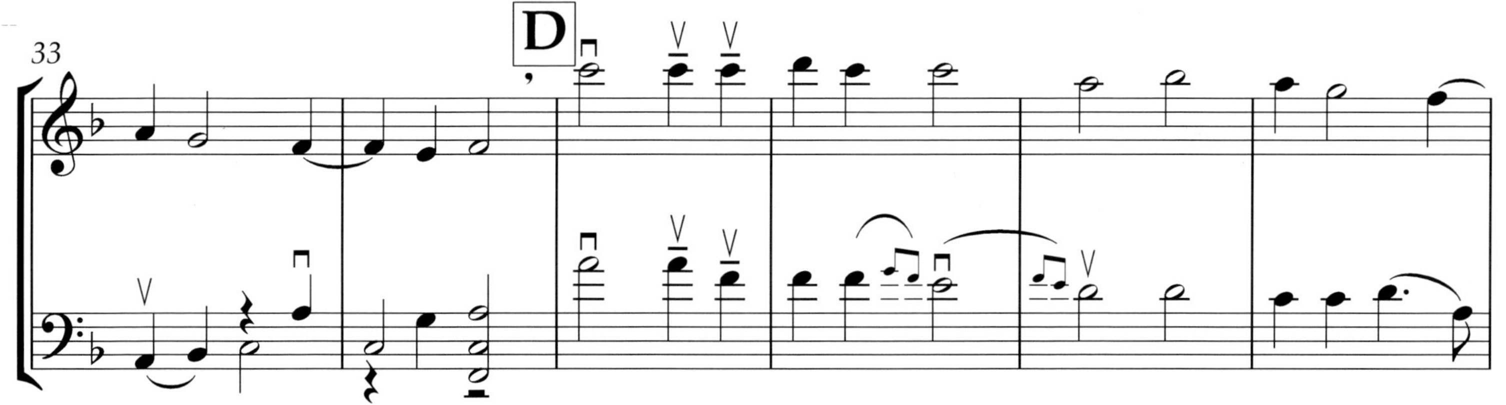
33
D

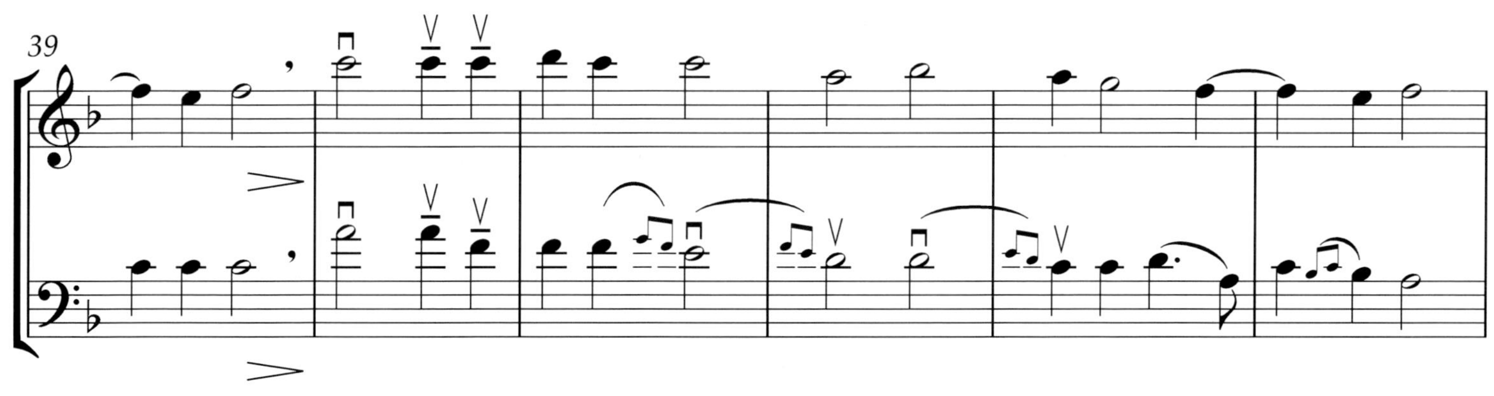
39

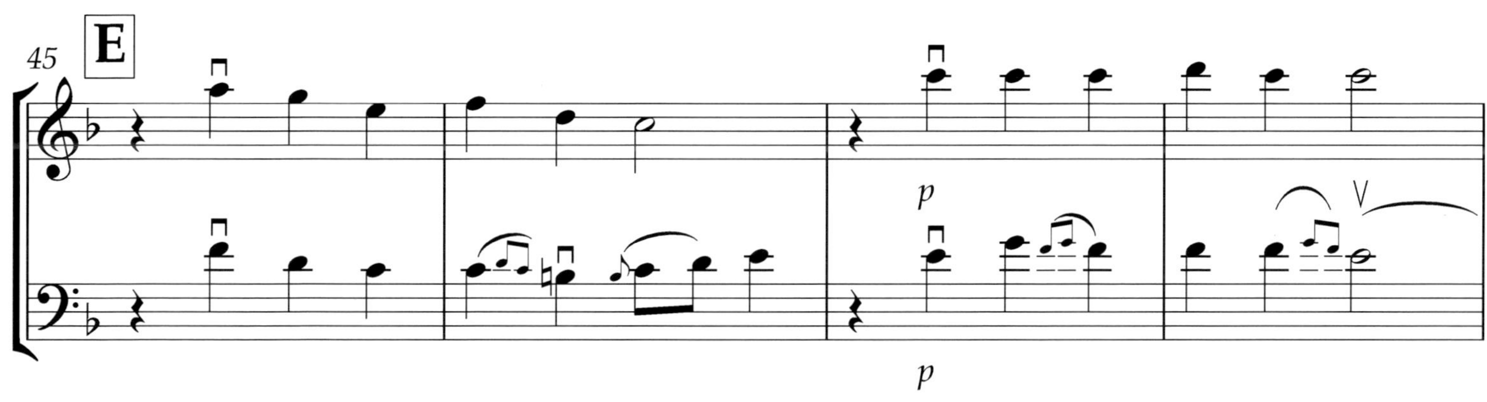
45
E
p
p

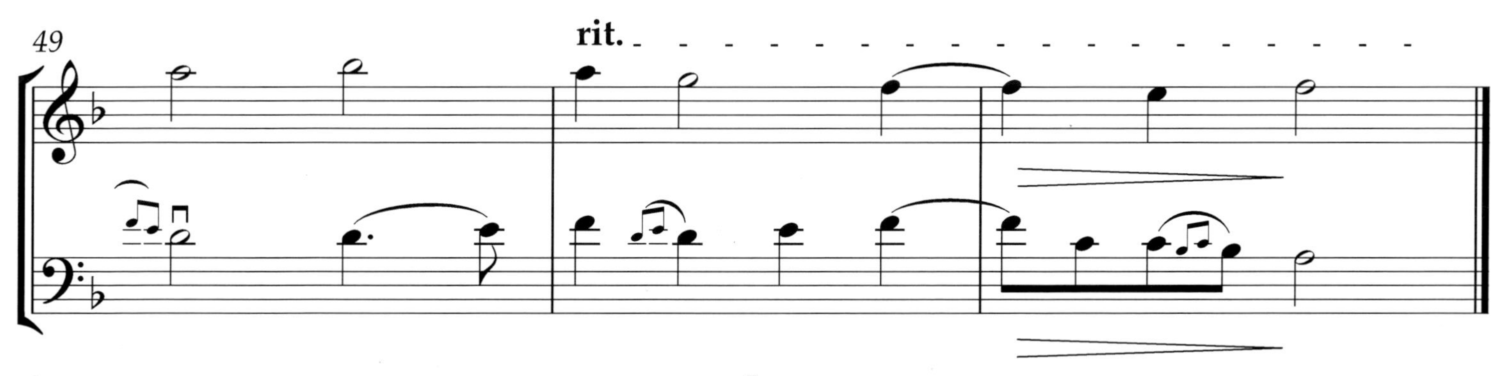
49
rit.

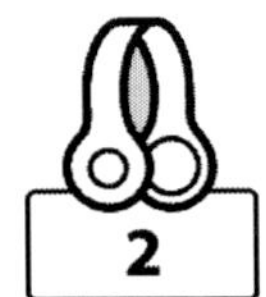


# *Coventry Carol*

Traditional
Arranged by The Wires: Sascha Groschang and Laurel Parks

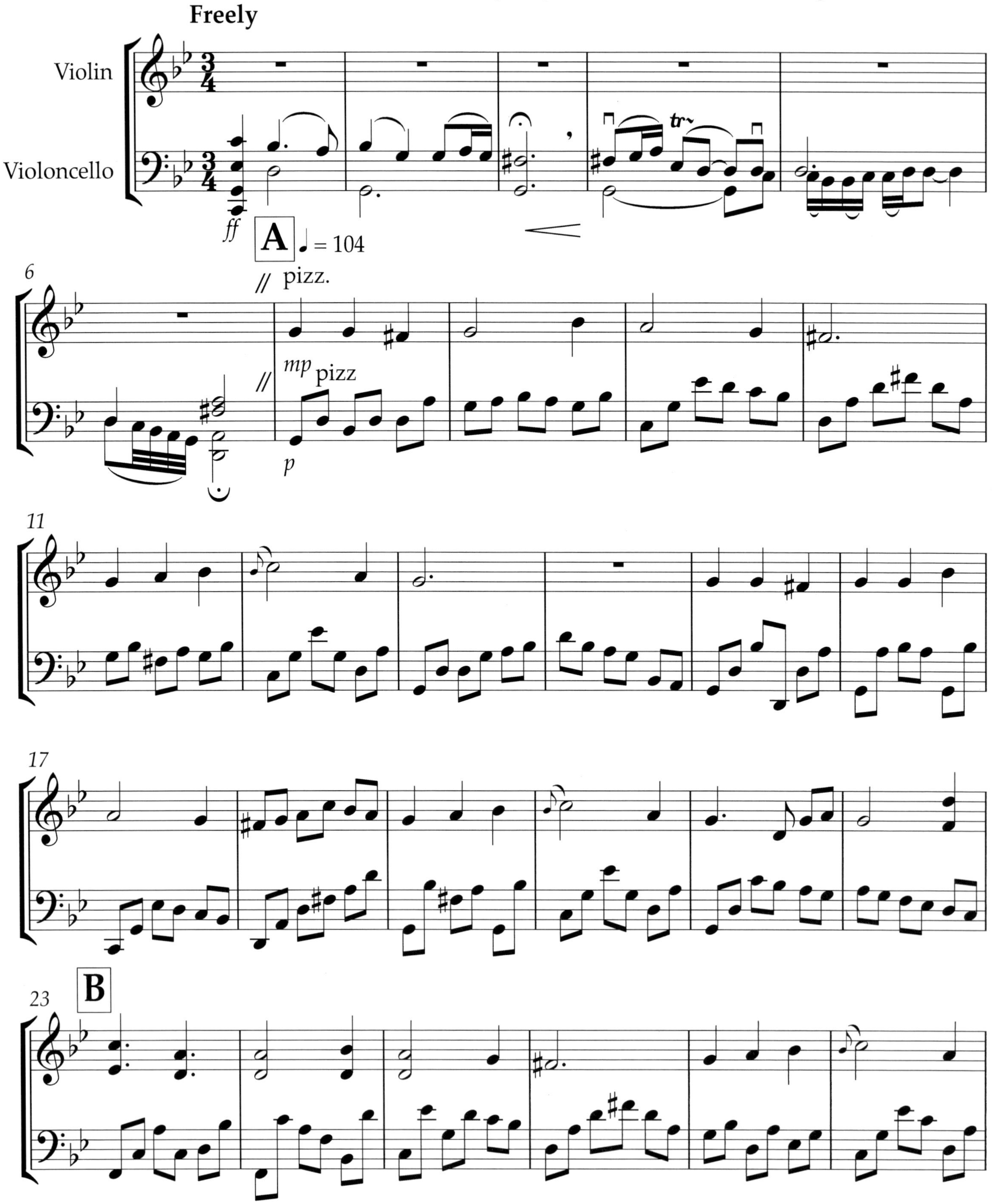

**Freely**

Violin

Violoncello

*ff*

A ♩ = 104

6

pizz.

*mp* pizz

*p*

11

17

23 B

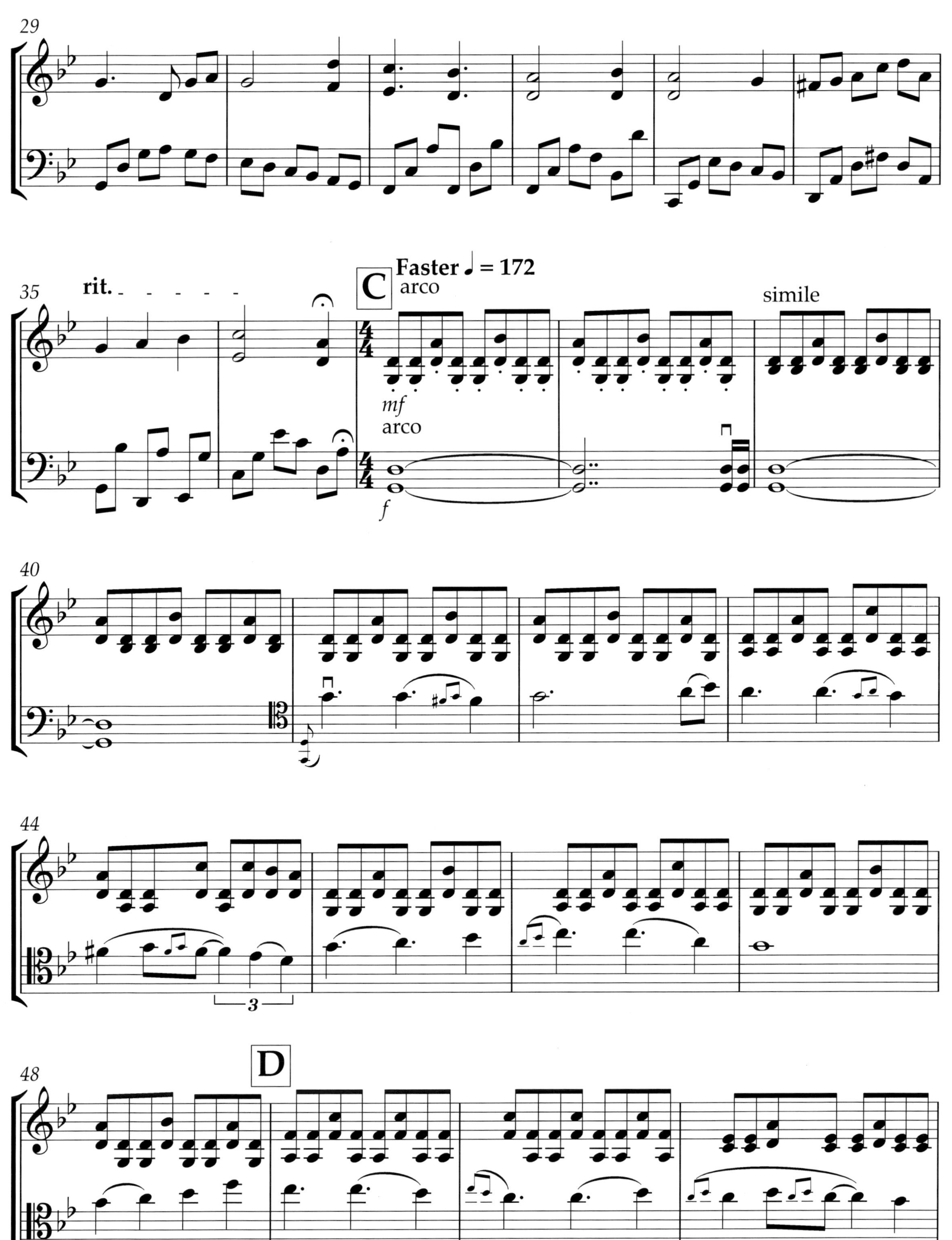
29
35
rit.
C
Faster ♩ = 172
arco
mf
arco
f
simile
40
44
3
48
D

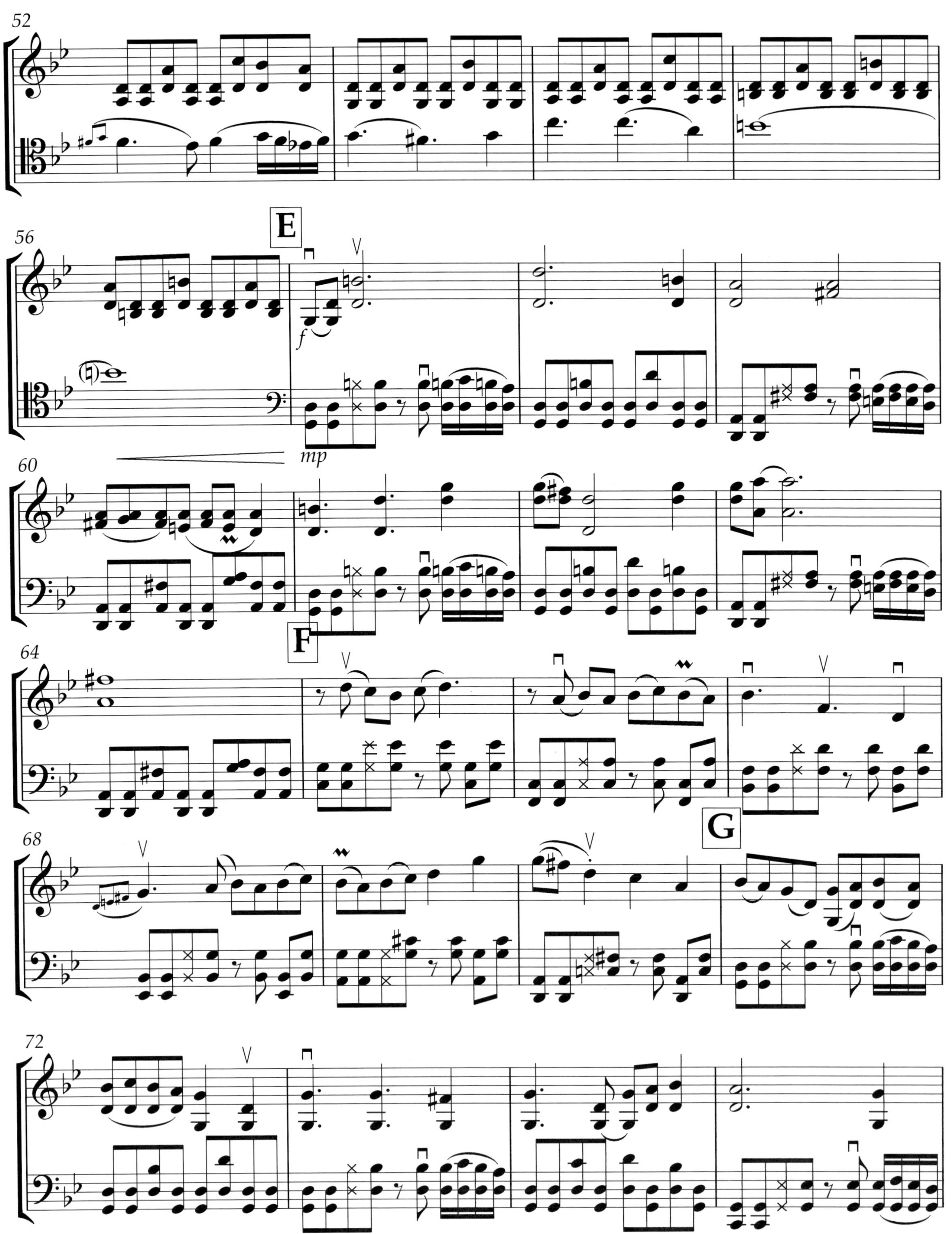

52
56
E
f
mp
60
F
64
68
G
72

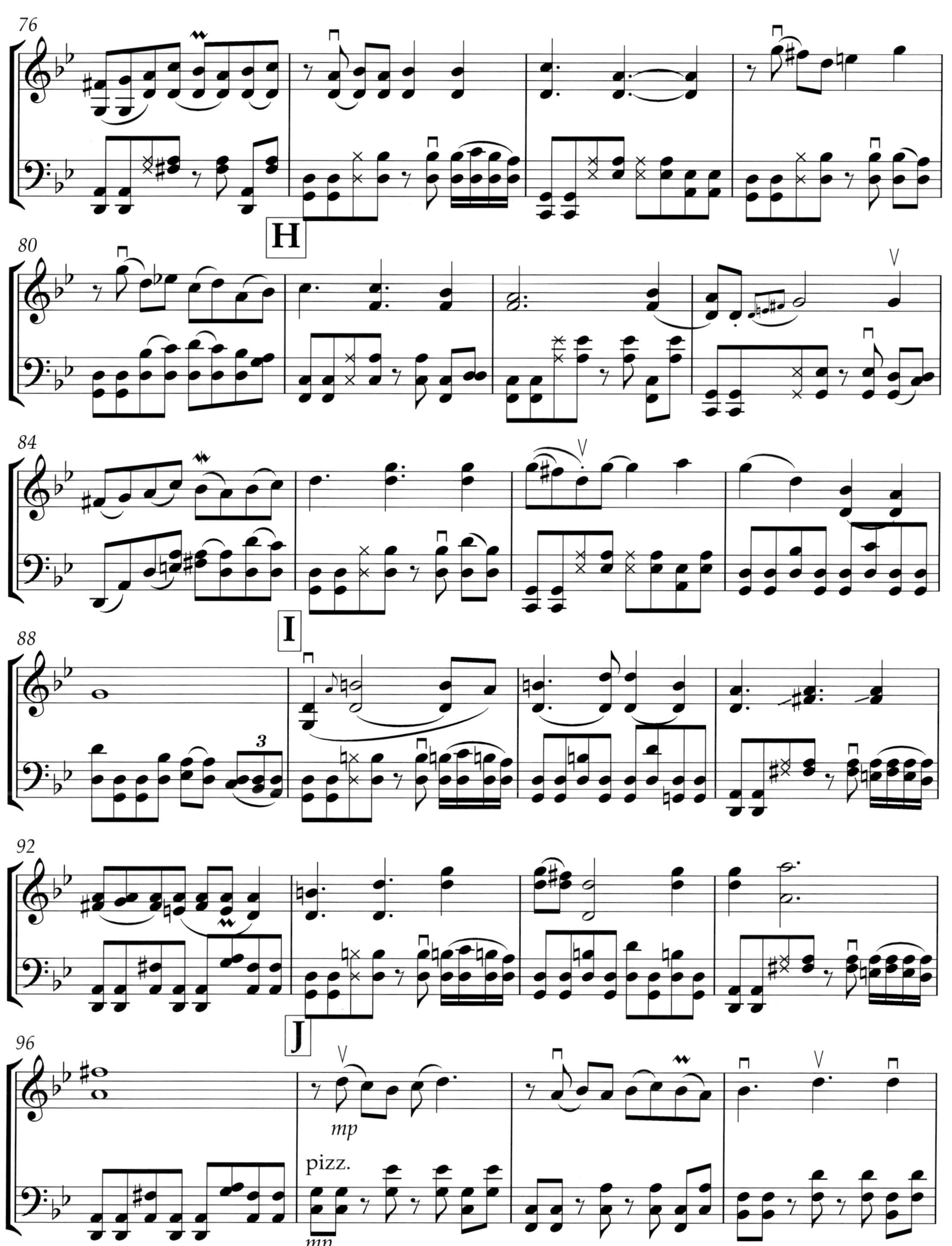
76
H
80
84
I
88
3
92
96
J
mp
pizz.
mp

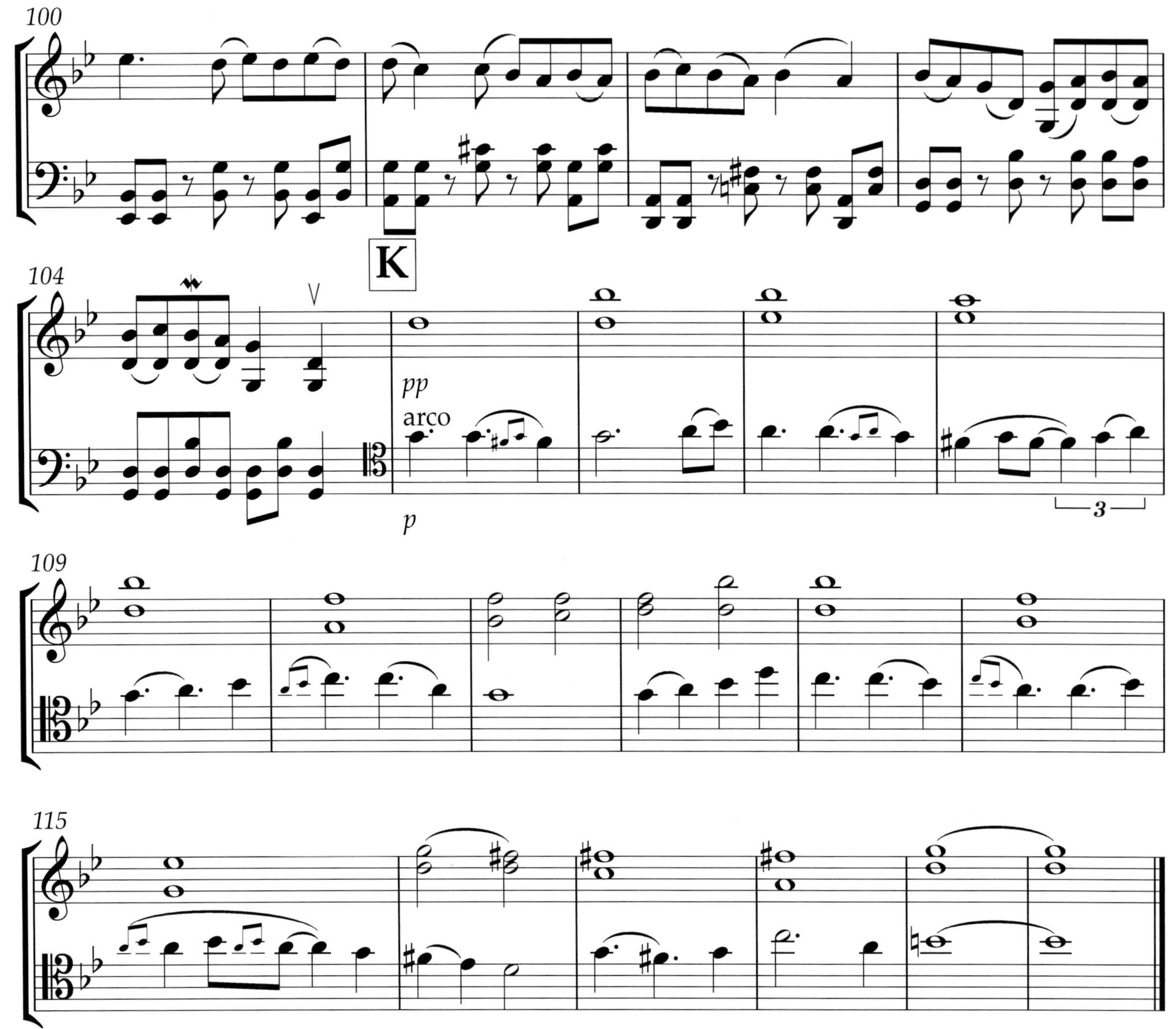
100
K
104
pp
arco
p
3
109
115

*This page has been left blank to avoid an awkward page turn.*

# *Silent Night*

Franz Xaver Gruber
Arranged by The Wires: Sascha Groschang and Laurel Parks

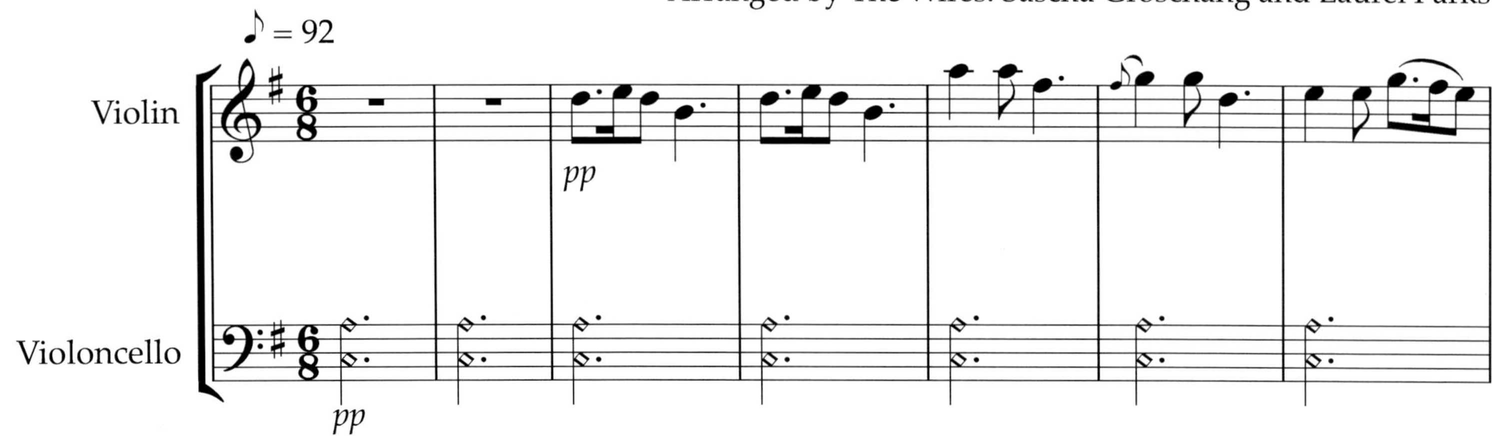

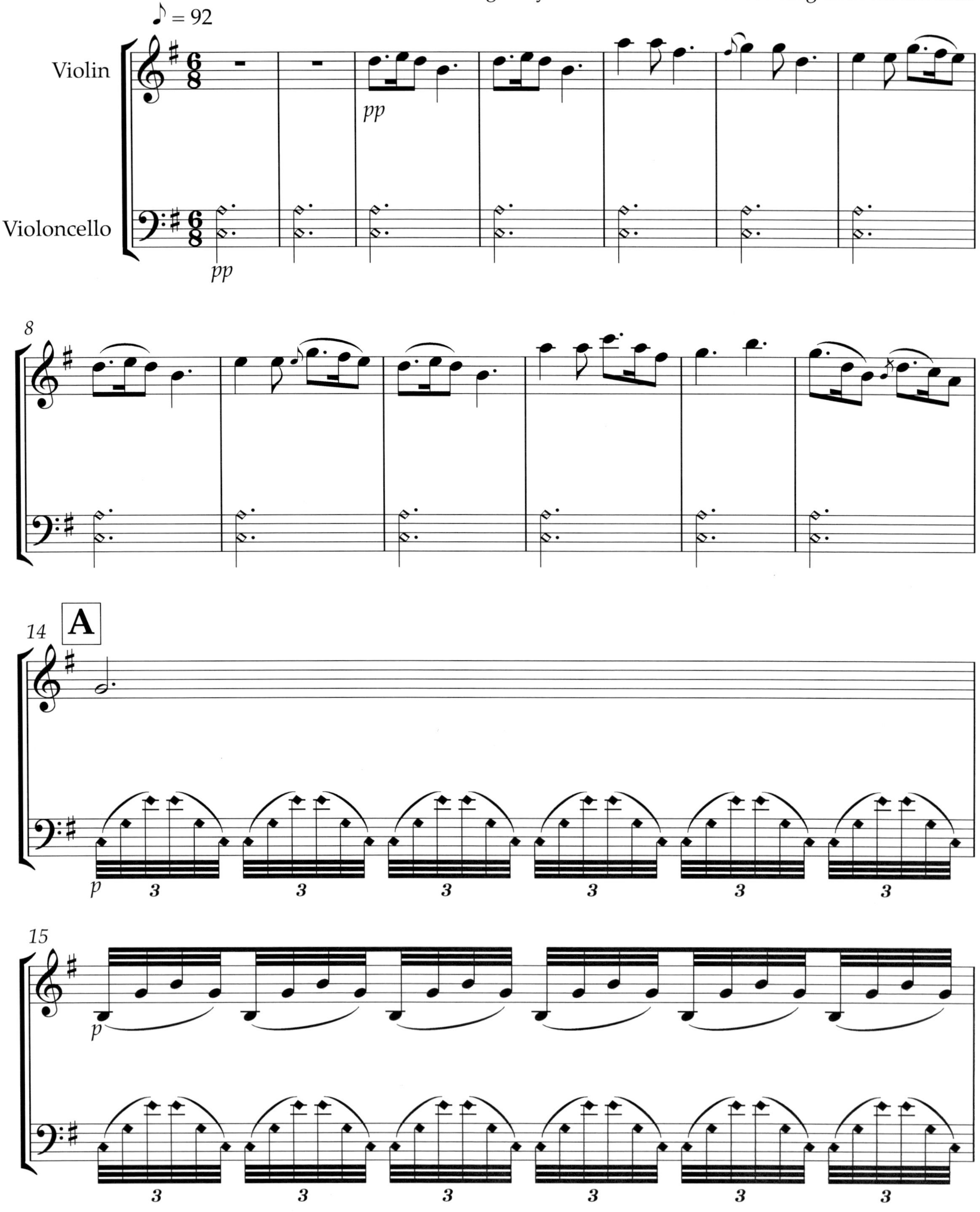

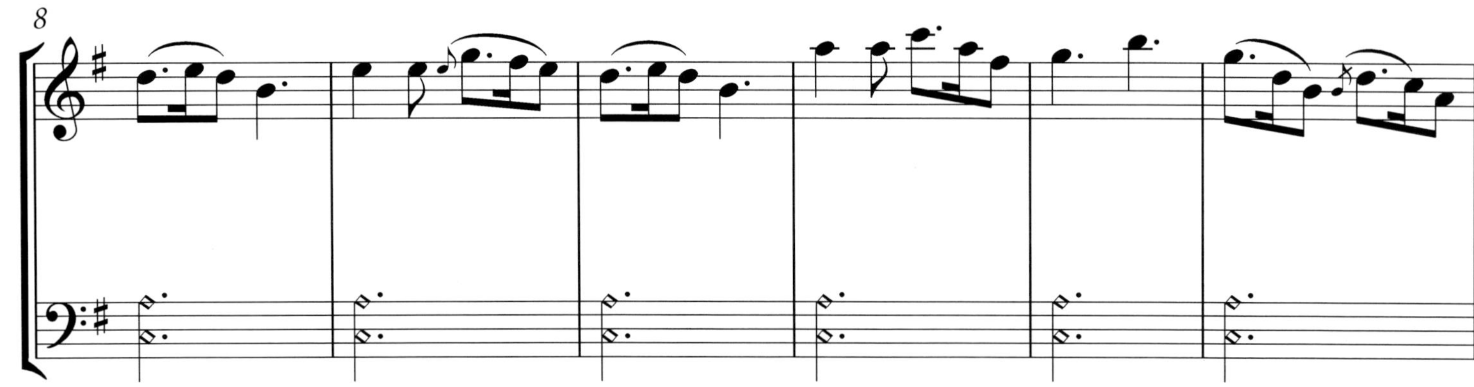


14 **A**

p

3 3 3 3 3 3

15

p

3 3 3 3 3 3

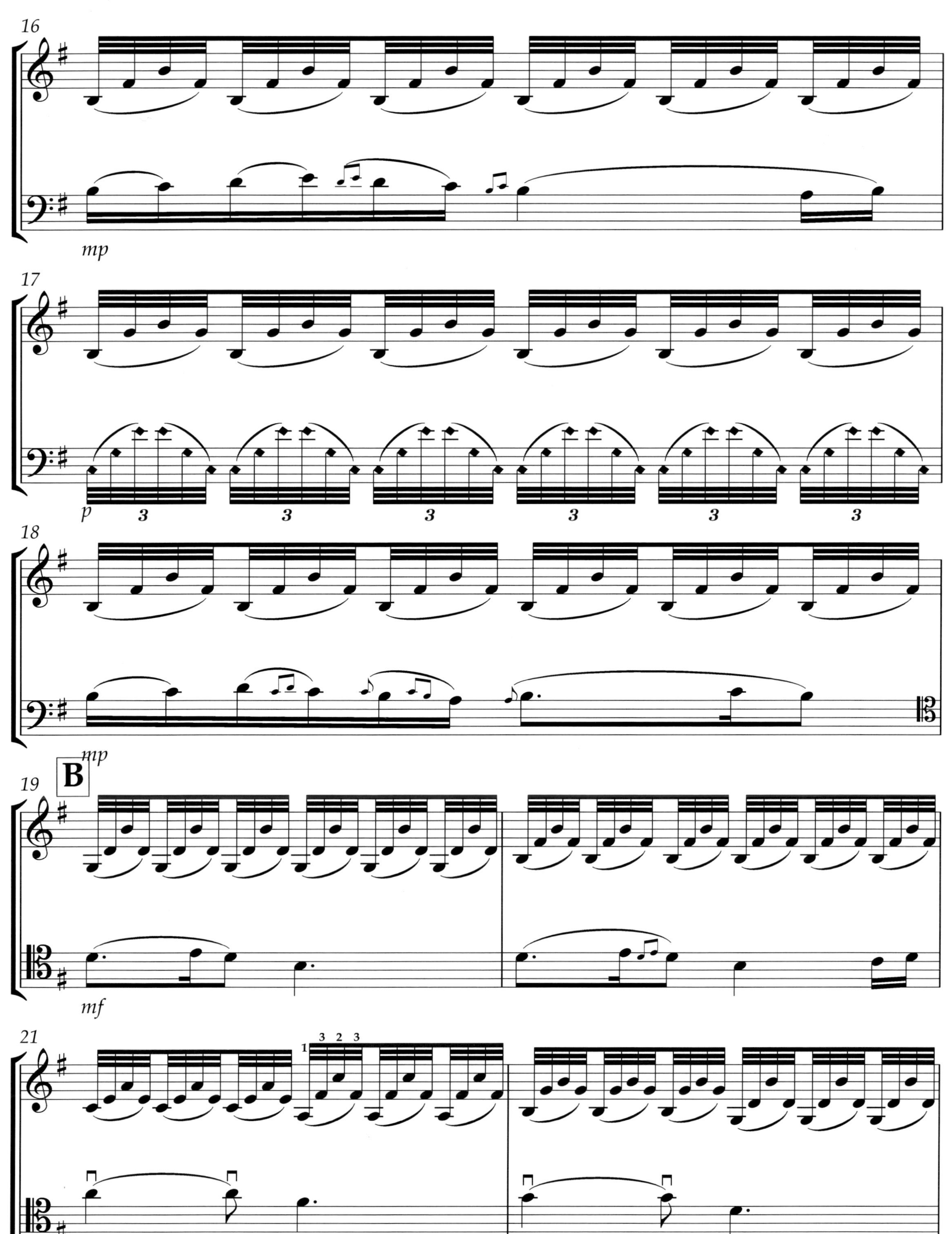
16
mp
17
p
3
18
mp
B
19
mf
21
1
3 2 3

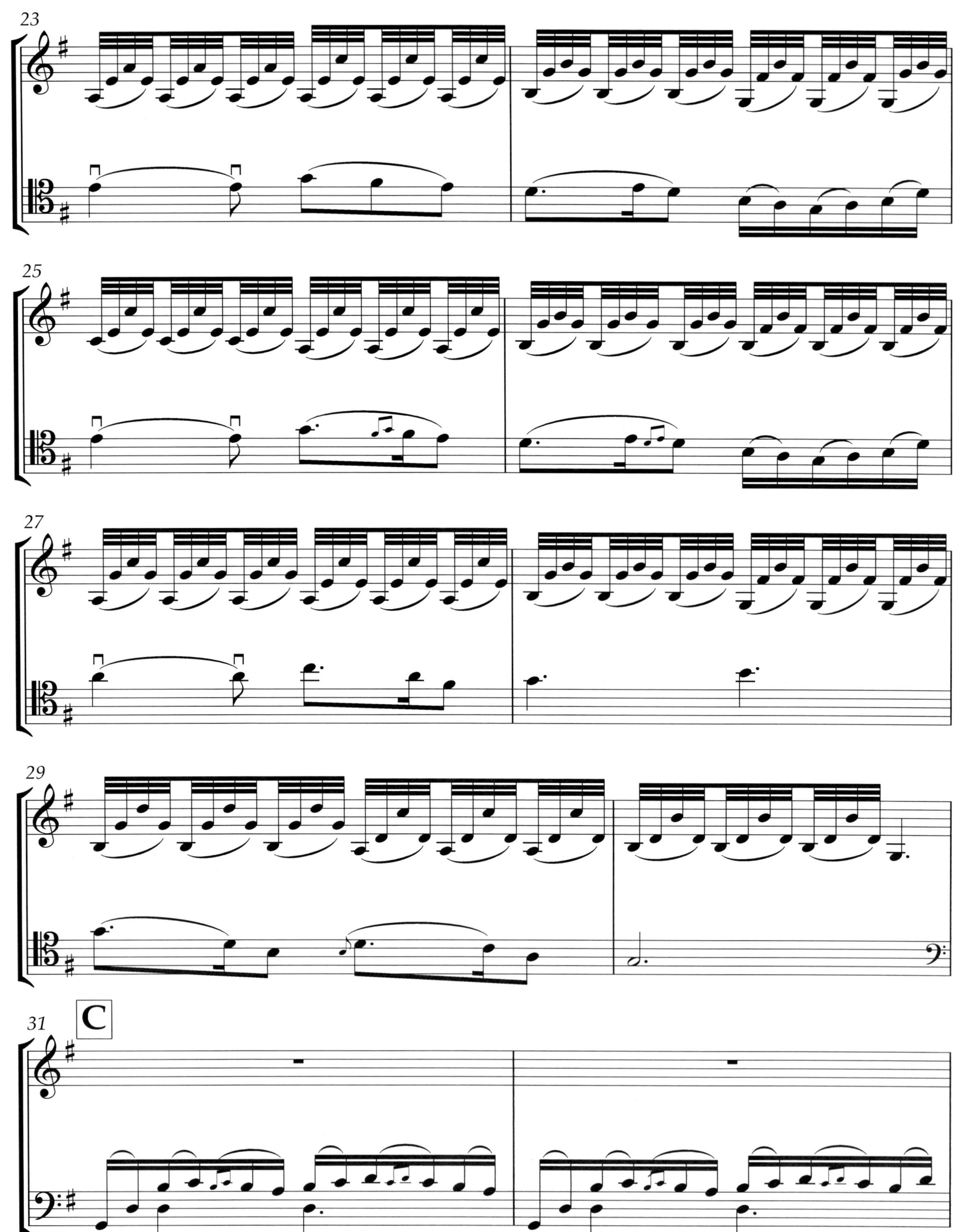
23
25
27
29
31
C

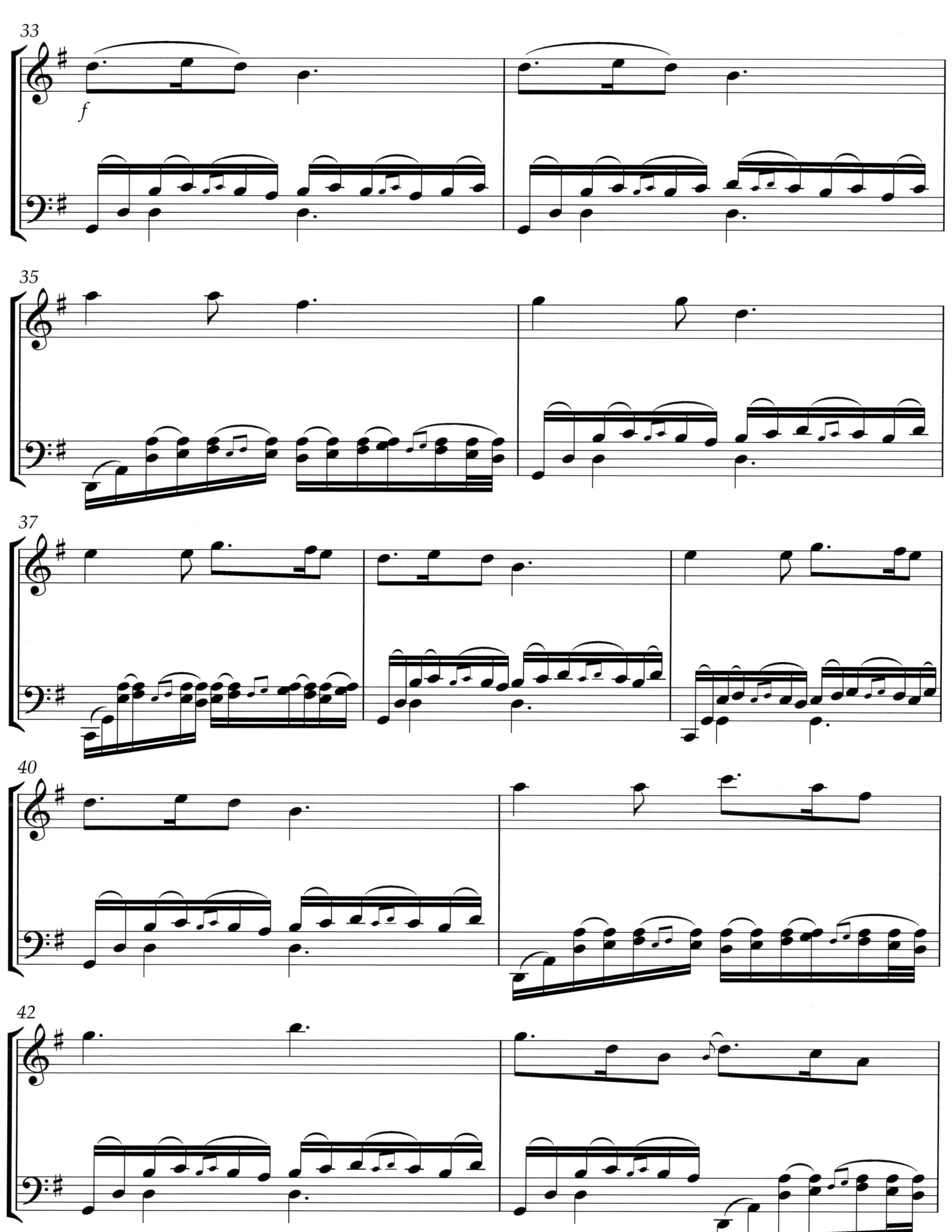
33
f
35
37
40
42

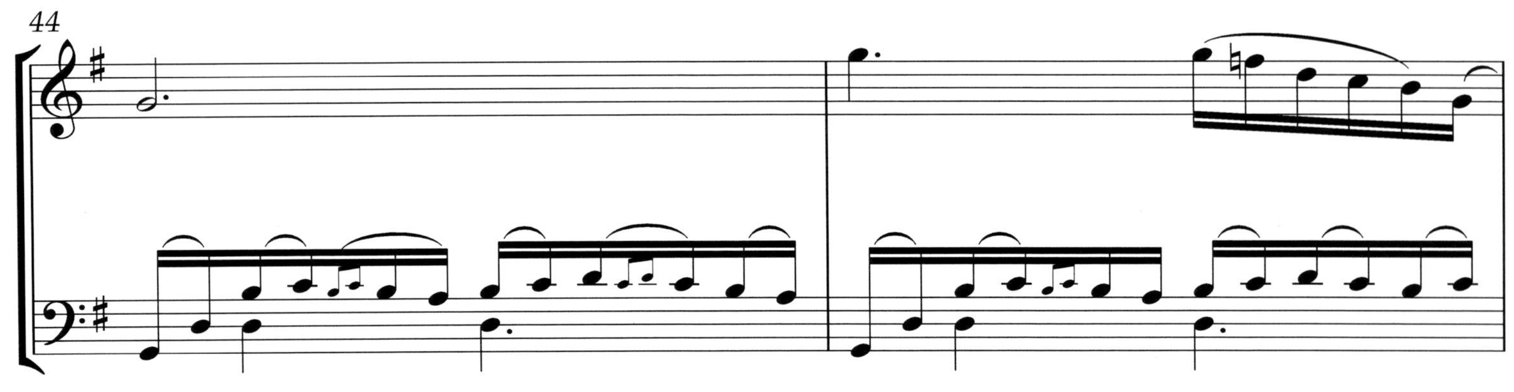
44

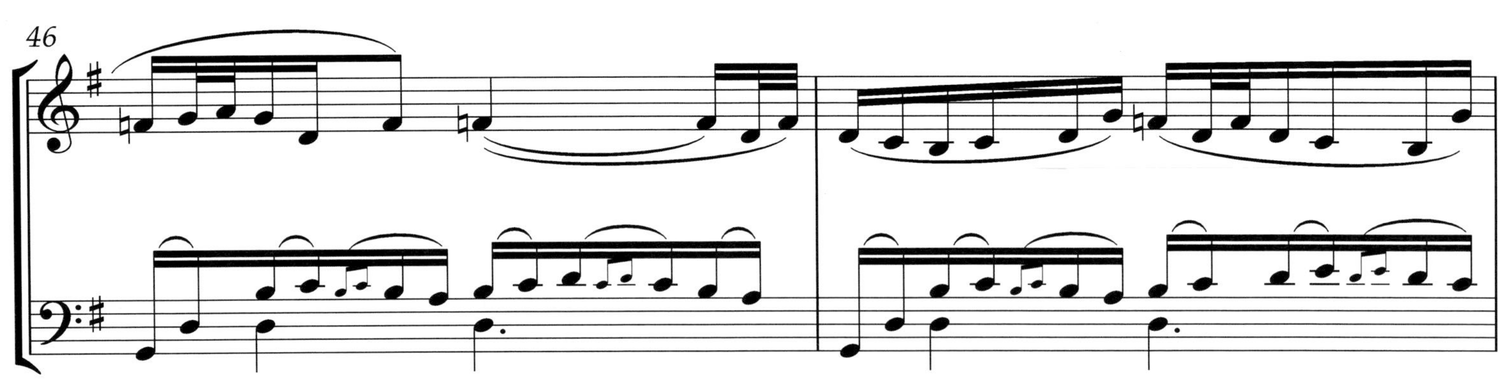
46

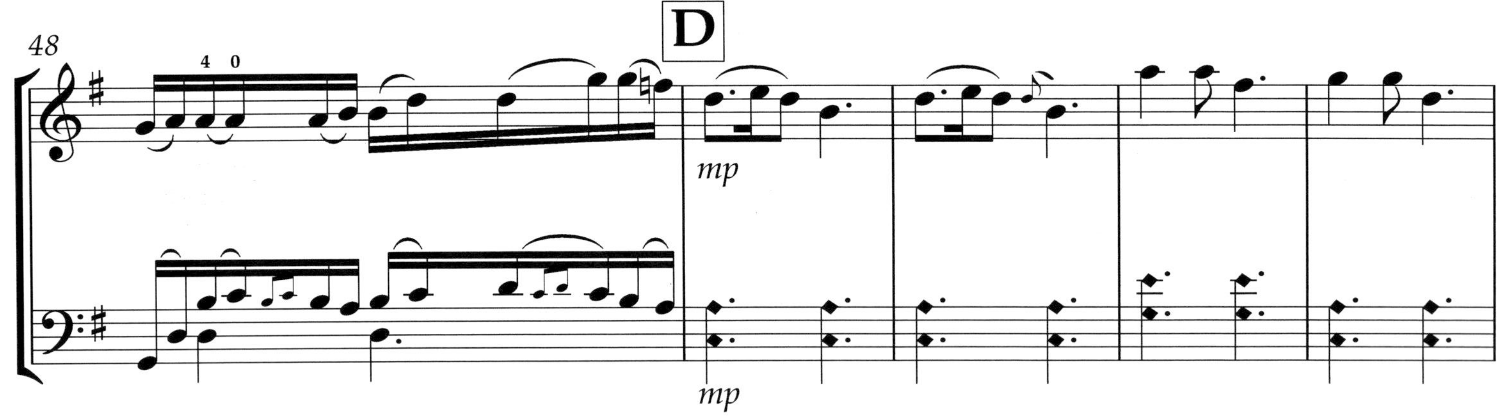
48
4
0
D
mp
mp

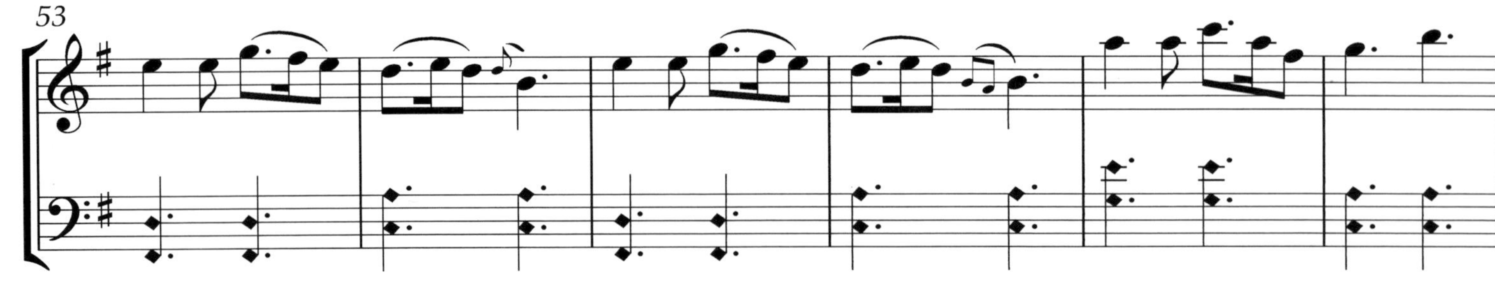
53

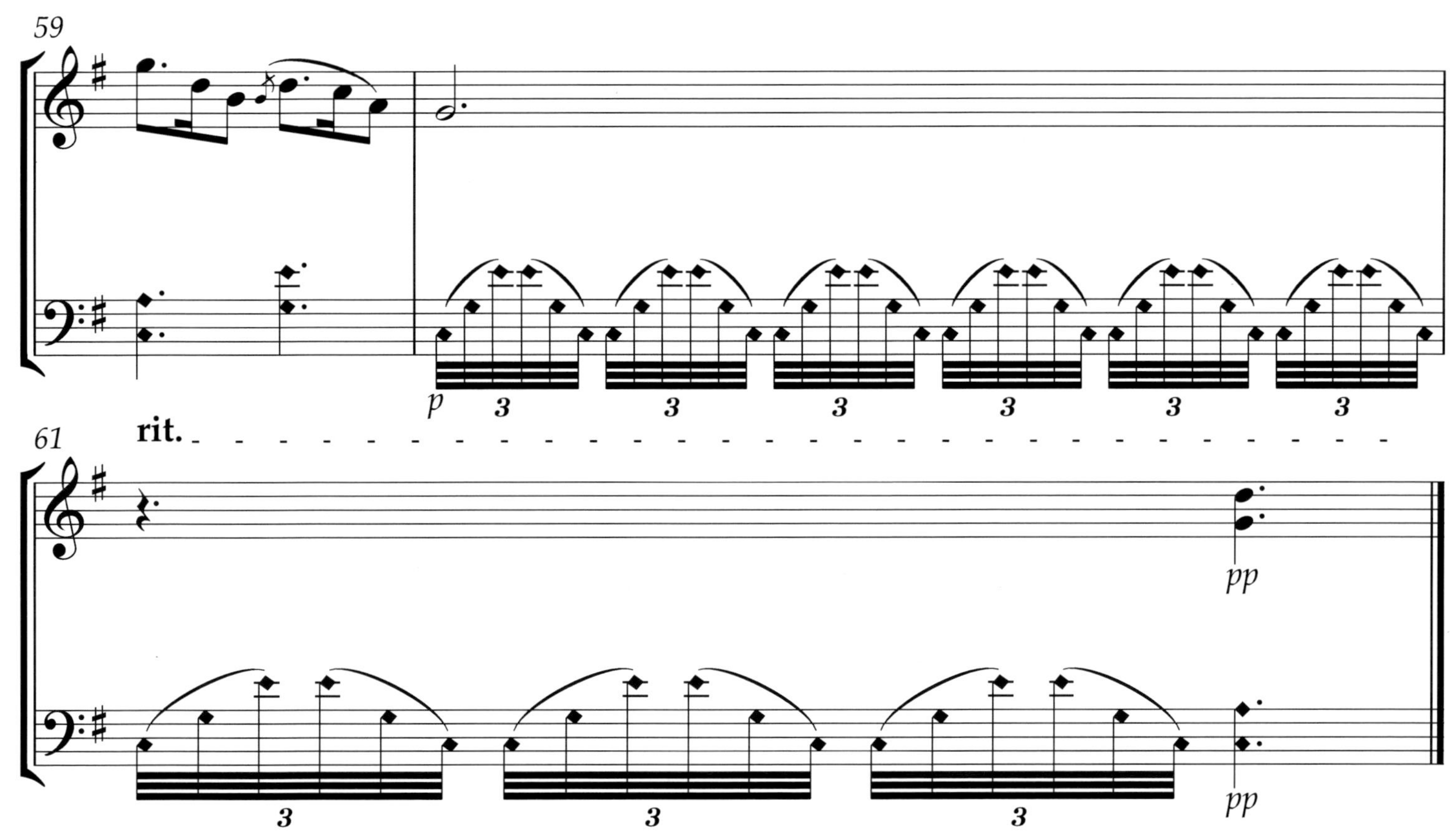
59
p
3
3
3
3
3
3
61
rit.
pp
3
3
3
pp

# Greensleeves

Traditional
Arranged by The Wires: Sascha Groschang and Laurel Parks

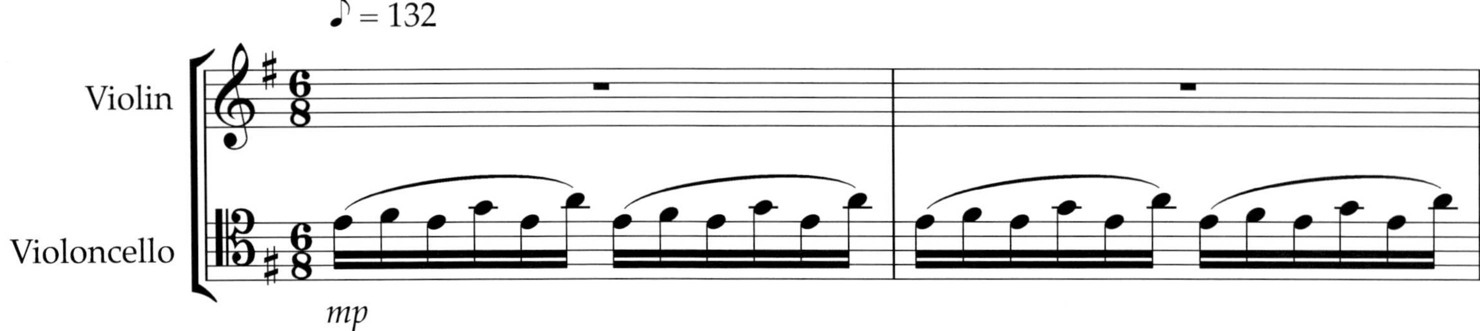


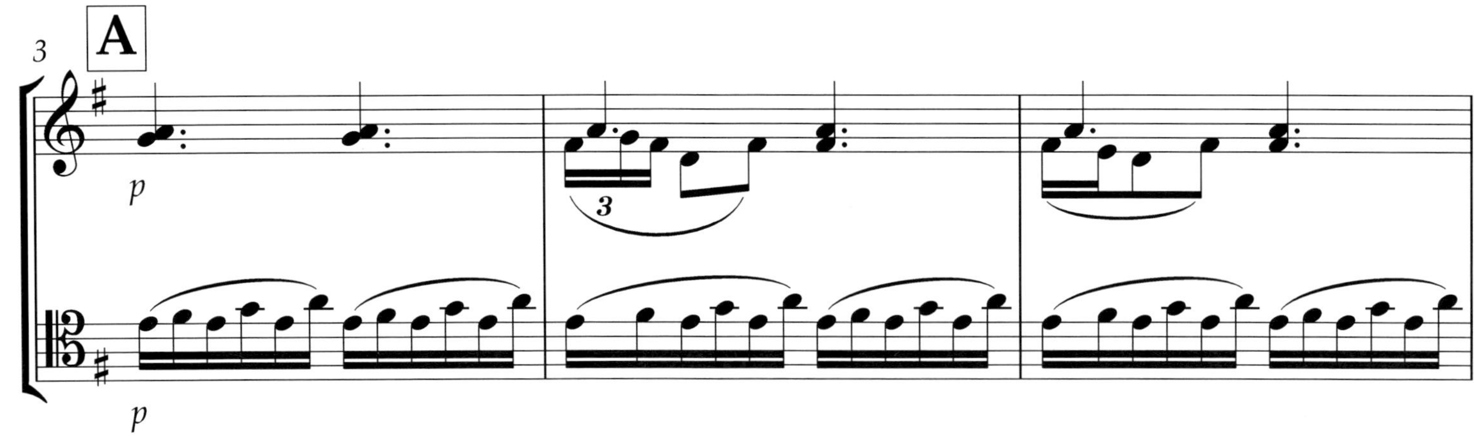


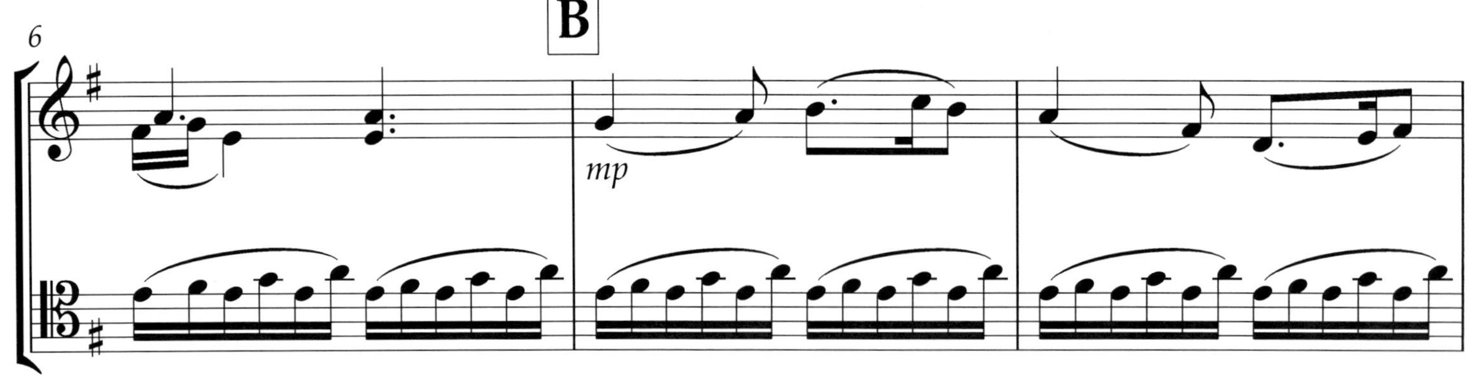


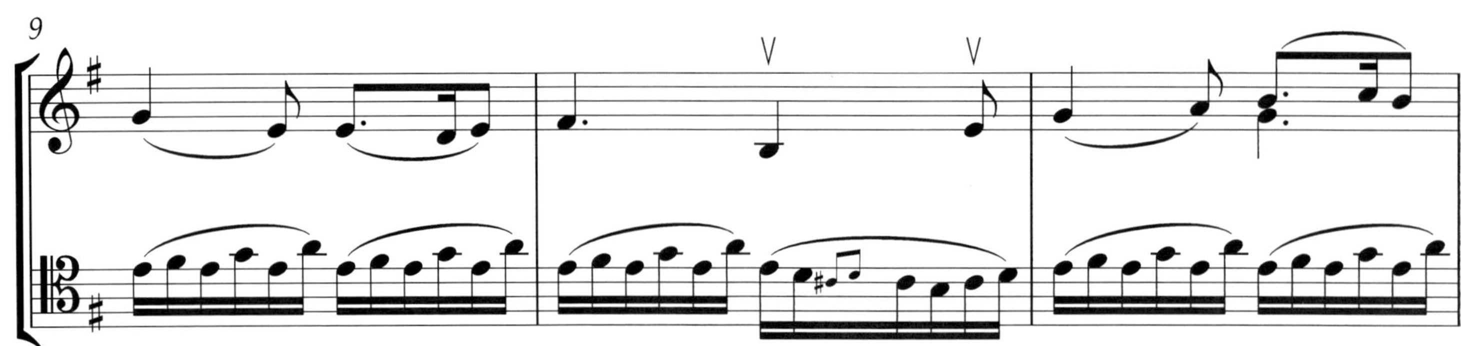

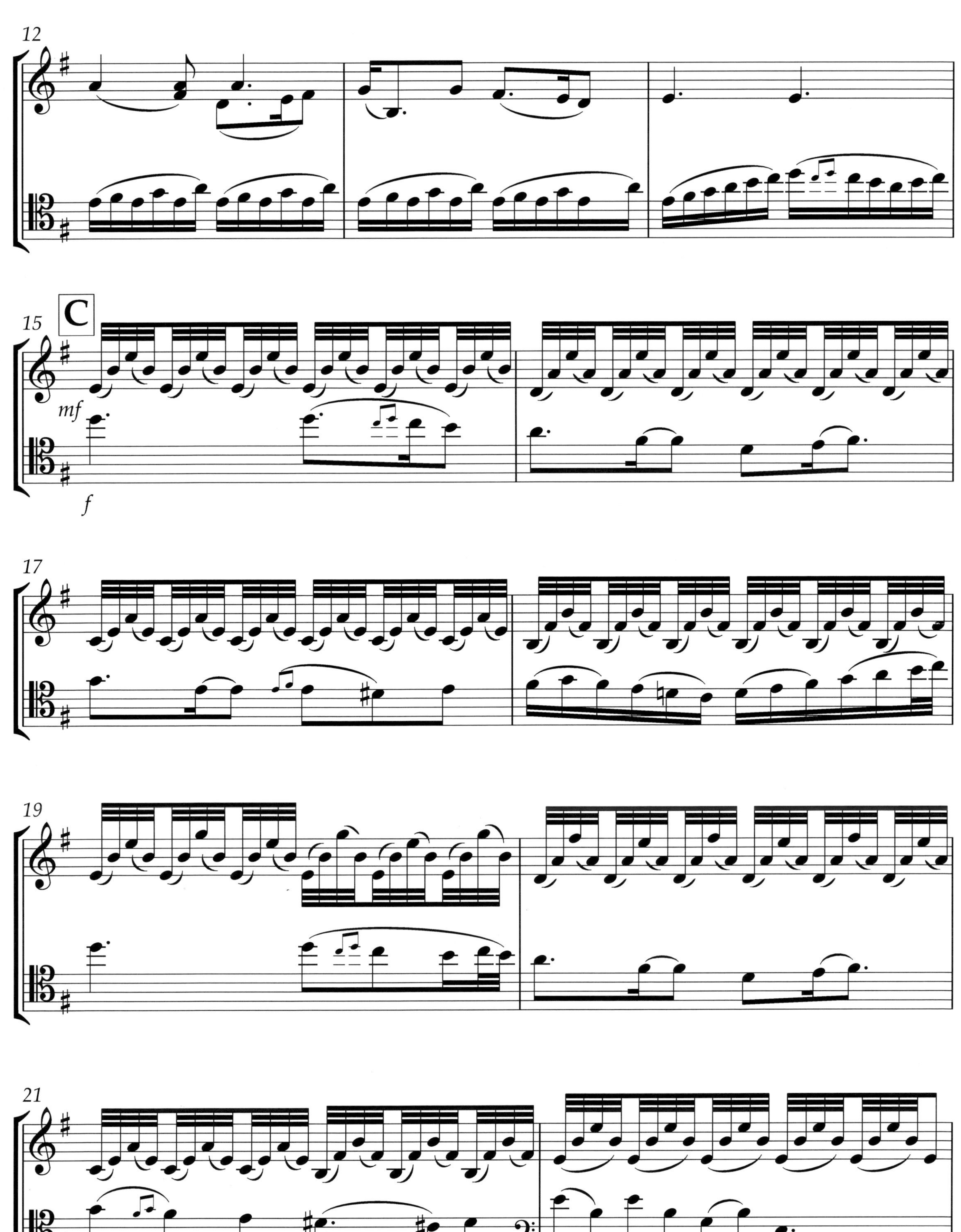
12
15
C
mf
f
17
19
21

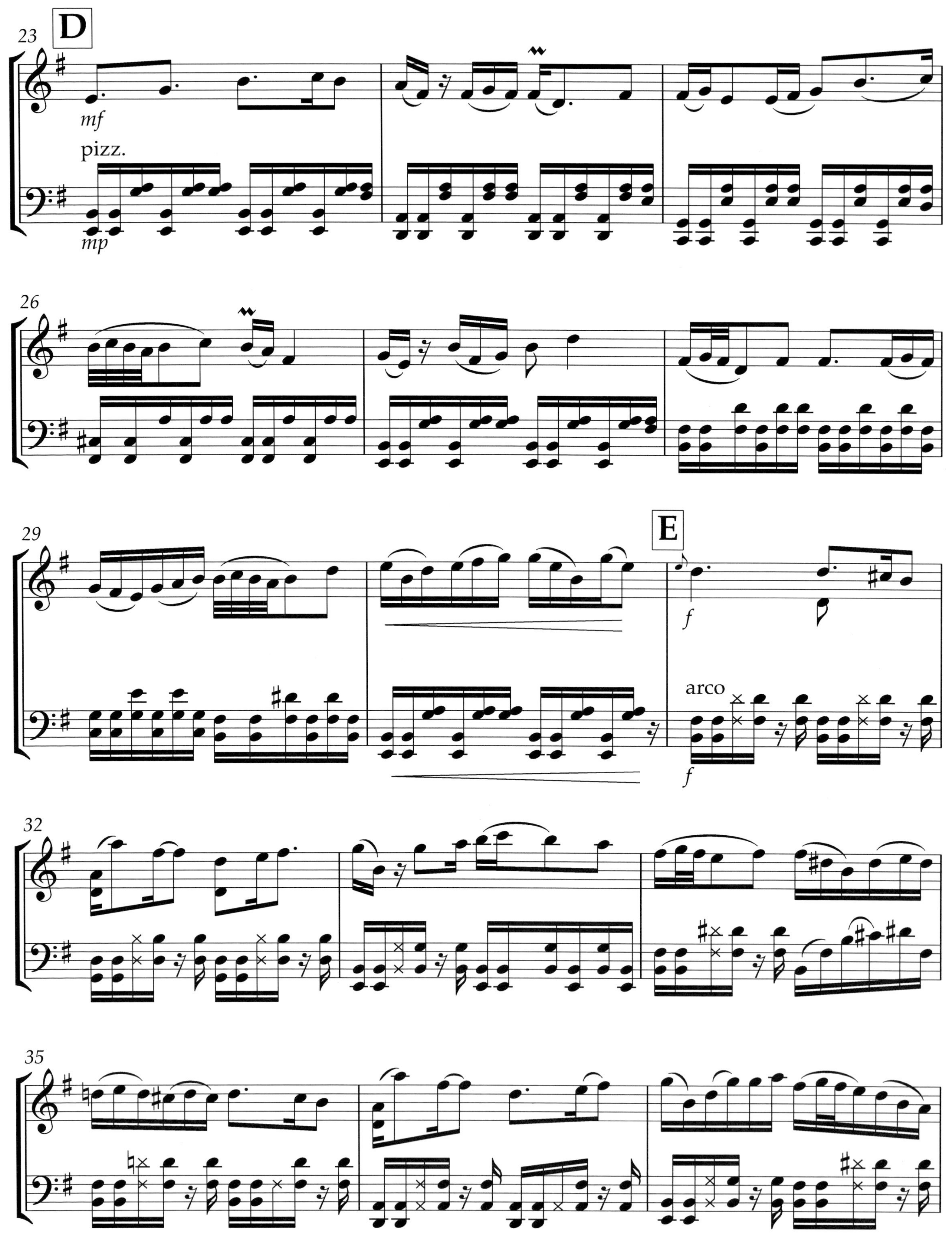

23
D
mf
pizz.
mp
26
29
E
f
arco
f
32
35

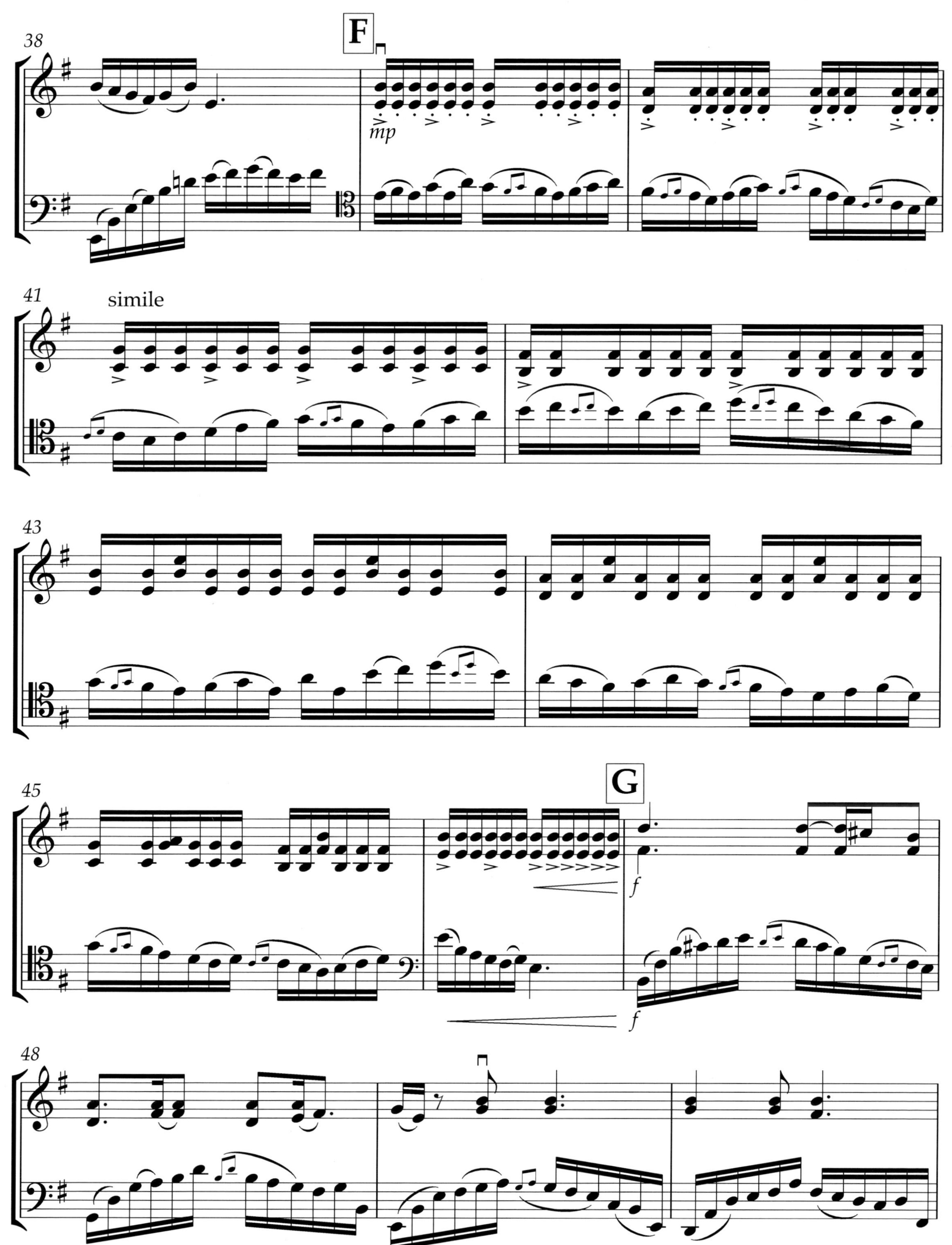
38
F
mp
41
simile
43
45
G
f
f
48

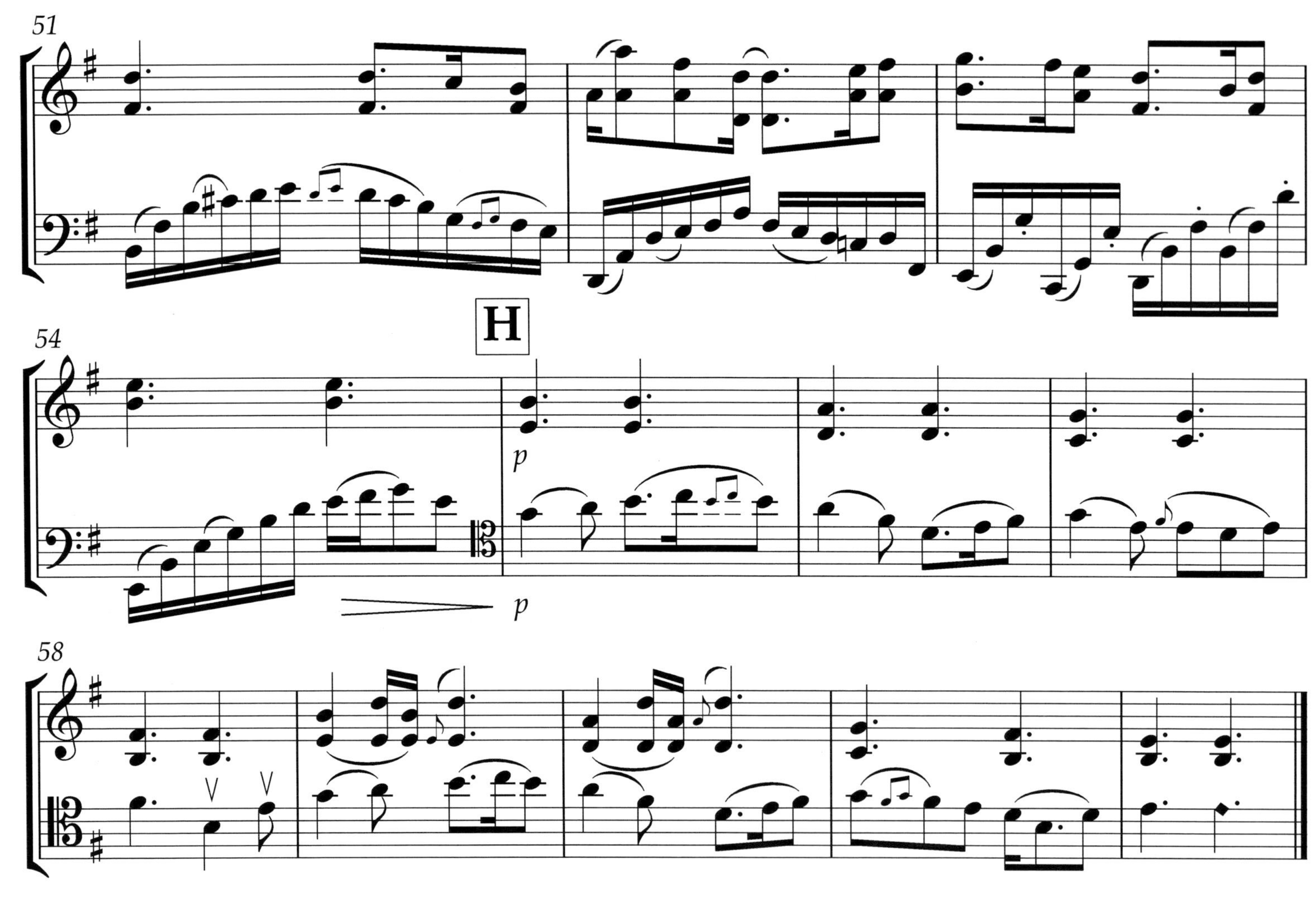
51
54
H
p
p
58

*This page has been left blank to avoid an awkward page turn.*

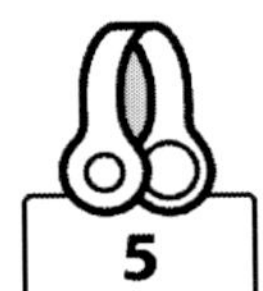


# The Holly and the Ivy

Arranged by The Wires: Sascha Groschang and Laurel Parks

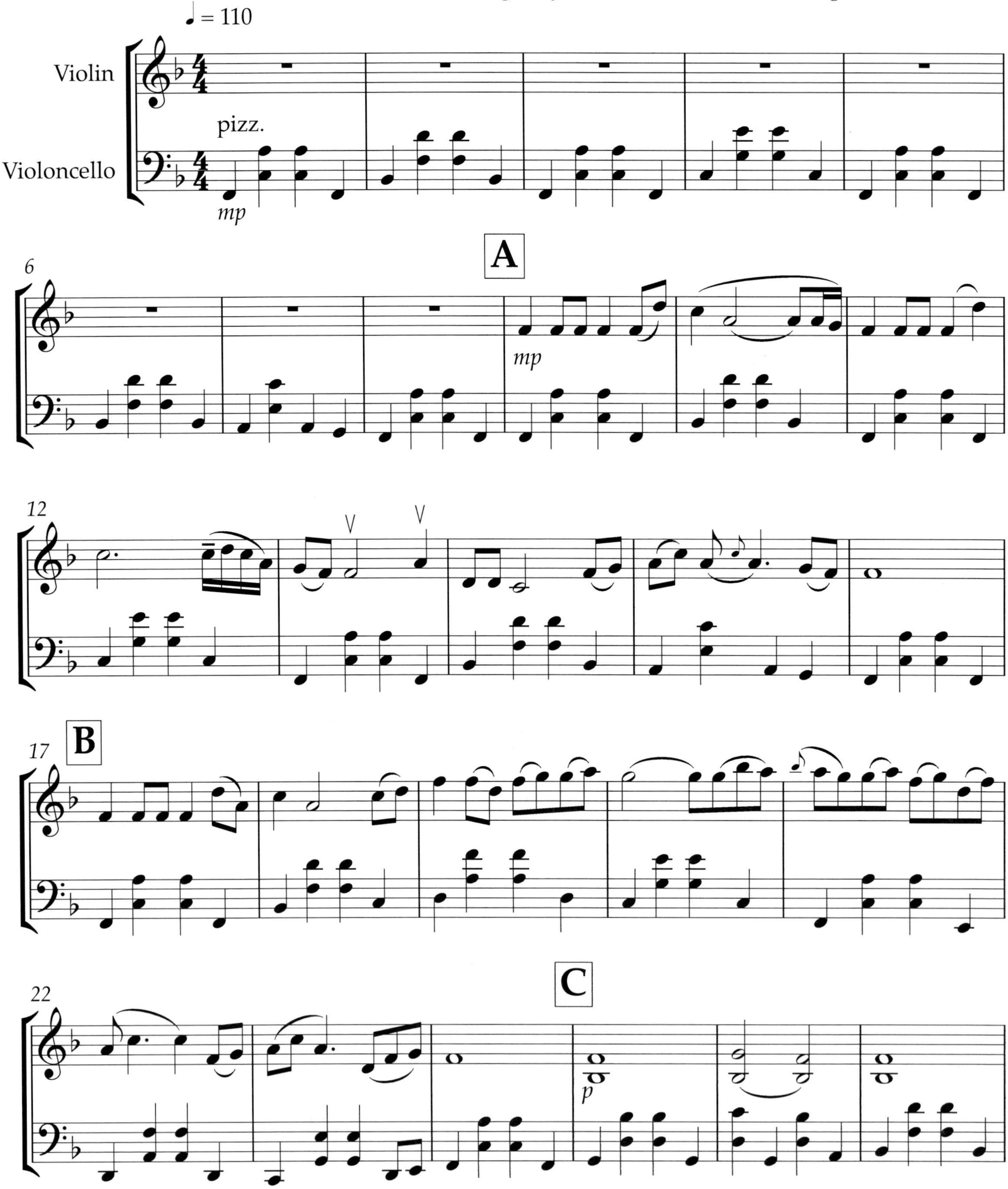

♩ = 110

Violin

Violoncello

pizz.

*mp*

6

A

*mp*

12

17 B

22

C

*p*

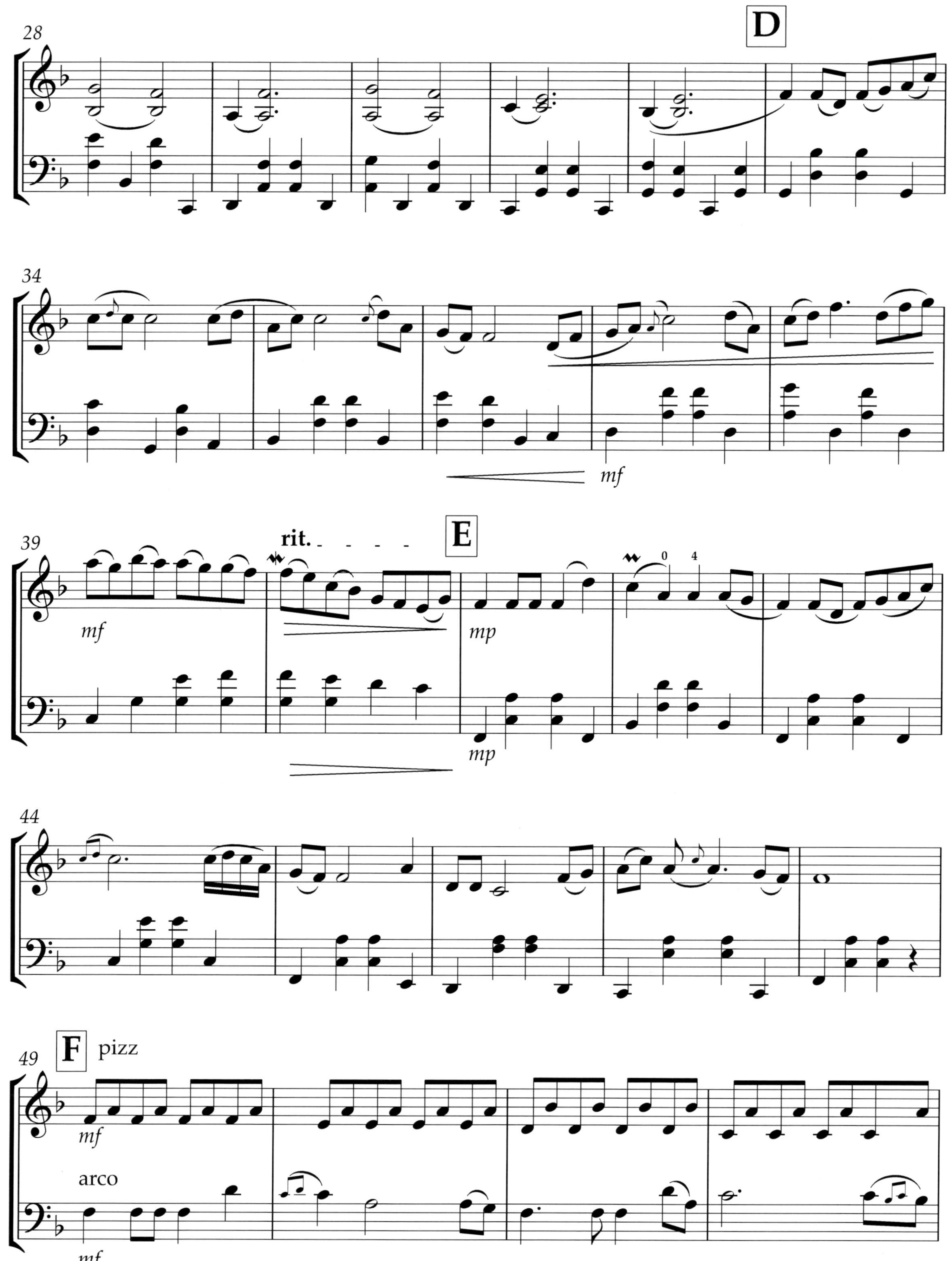

D
rit.
E
F
pizz
arco
mf
mp

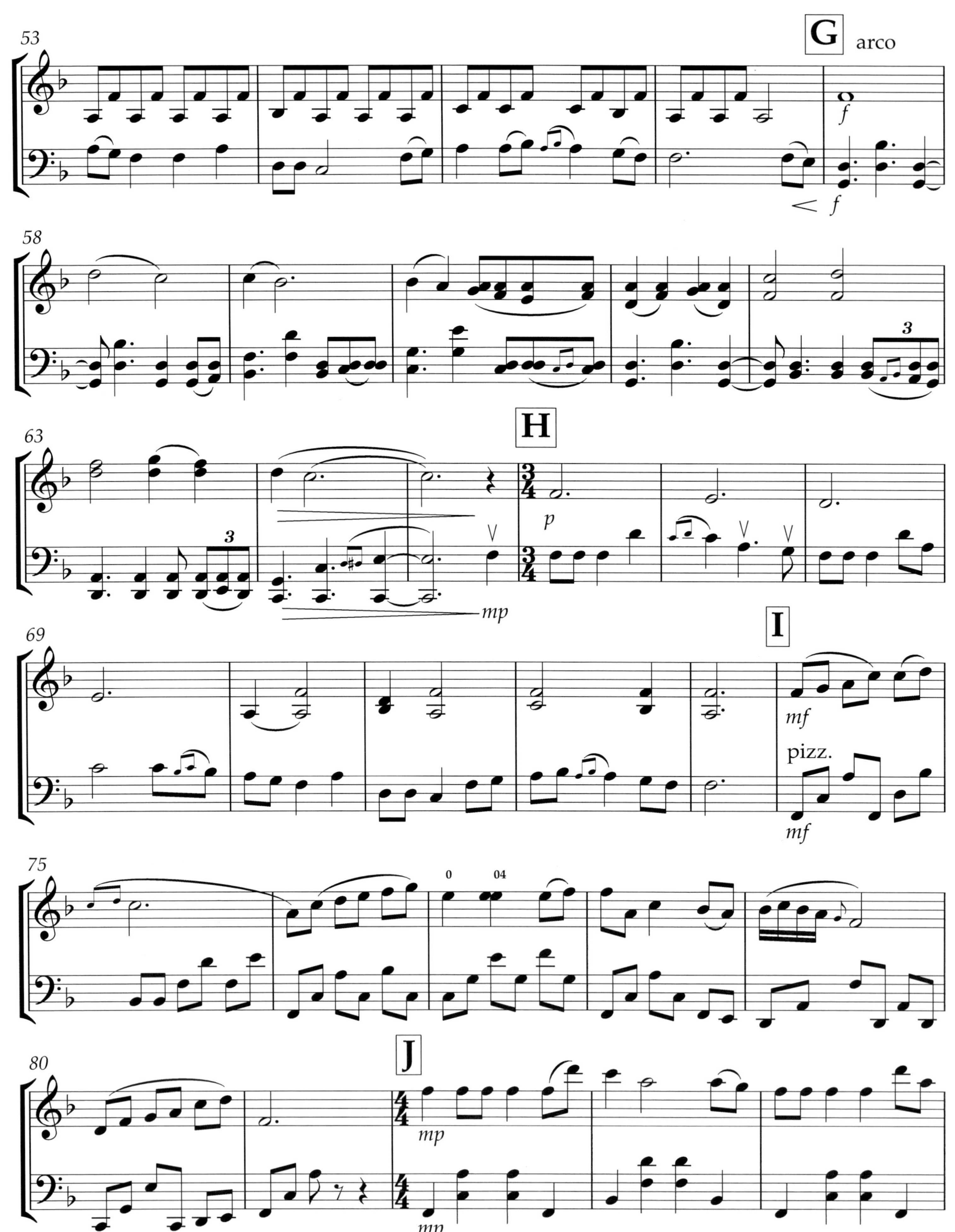
53
G
arco
f
f
58
3
63
H
3
p
mp
69
I
mf
pizz.
mf
75
0
04
80
J
mp
mp

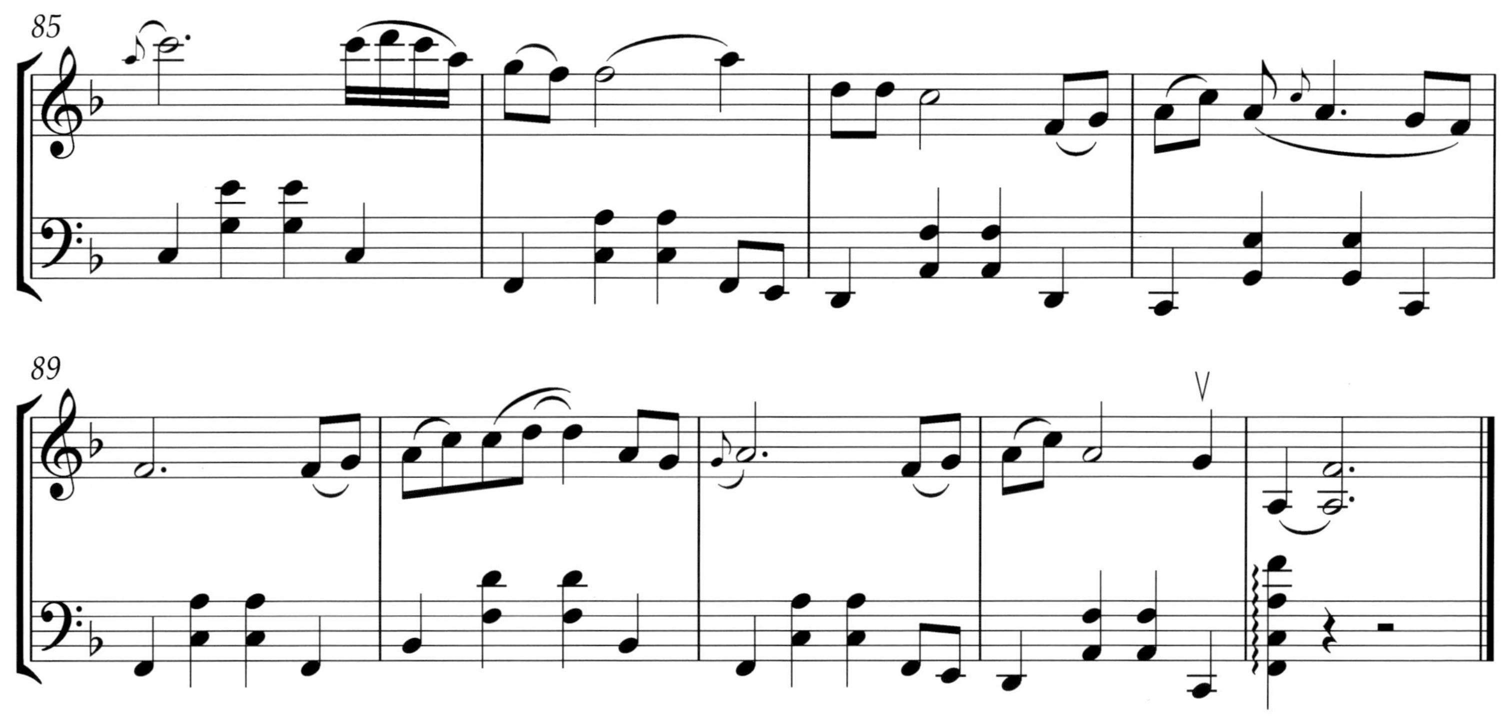
85
89

# *Wexford Carol*

Tradtional English
Arranged by The Wires: Sascha Groschang and Laurel Parks

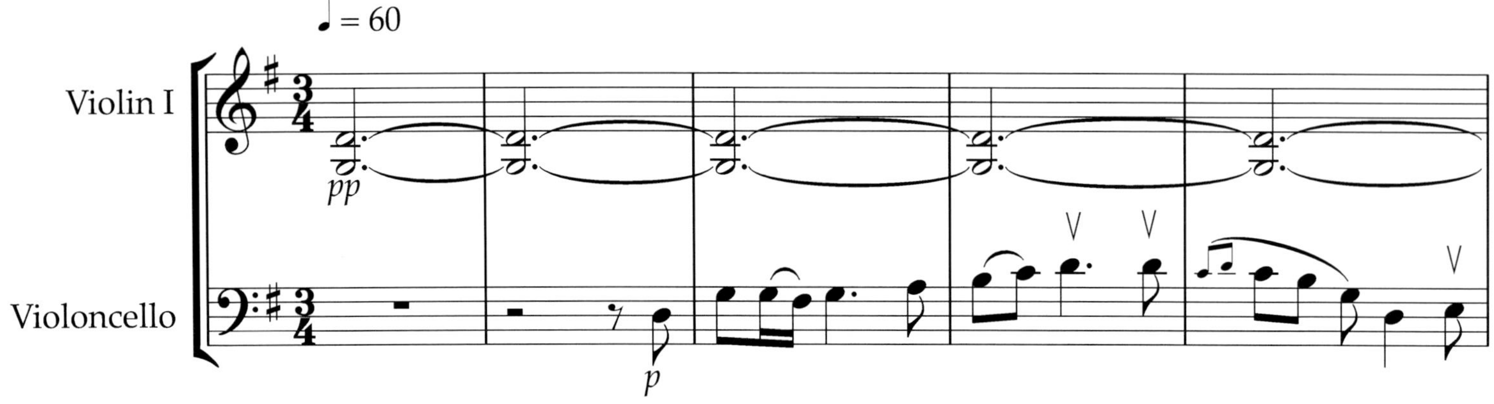


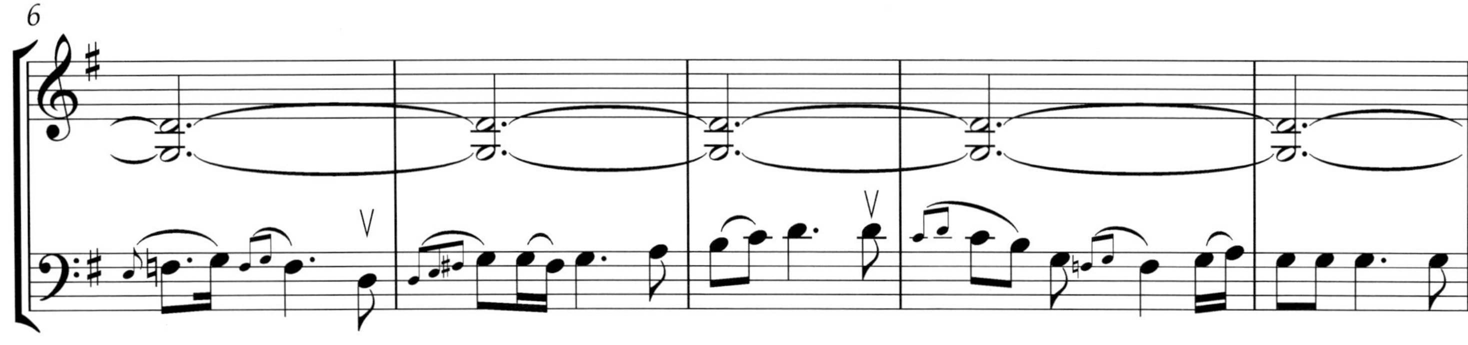


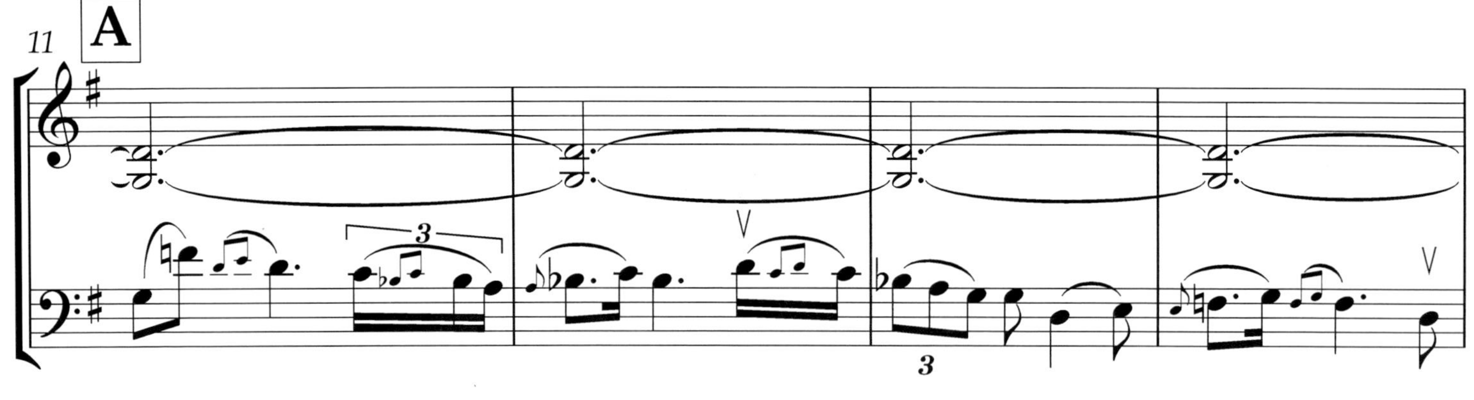


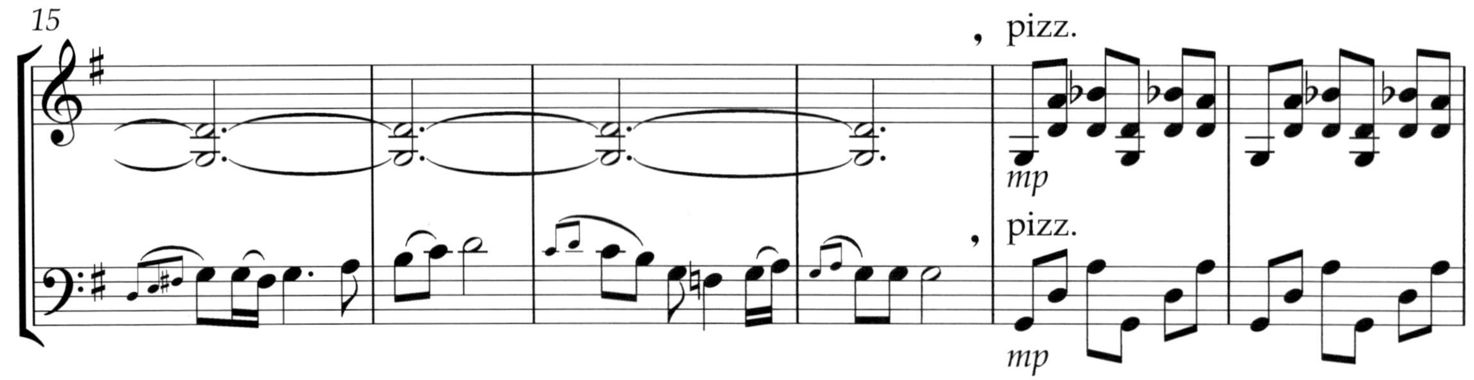

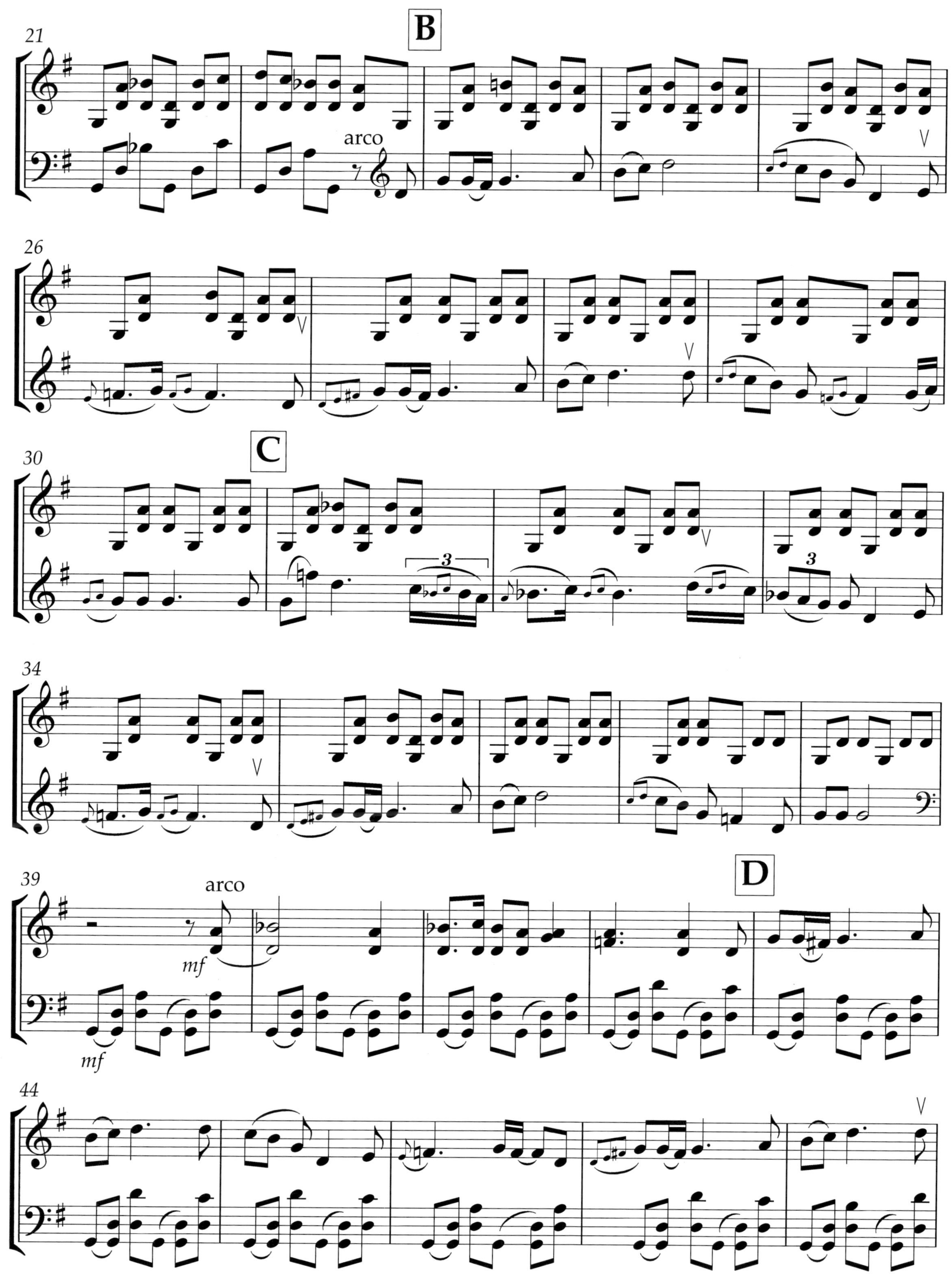
B
arco
C
arco
mf
mf
D

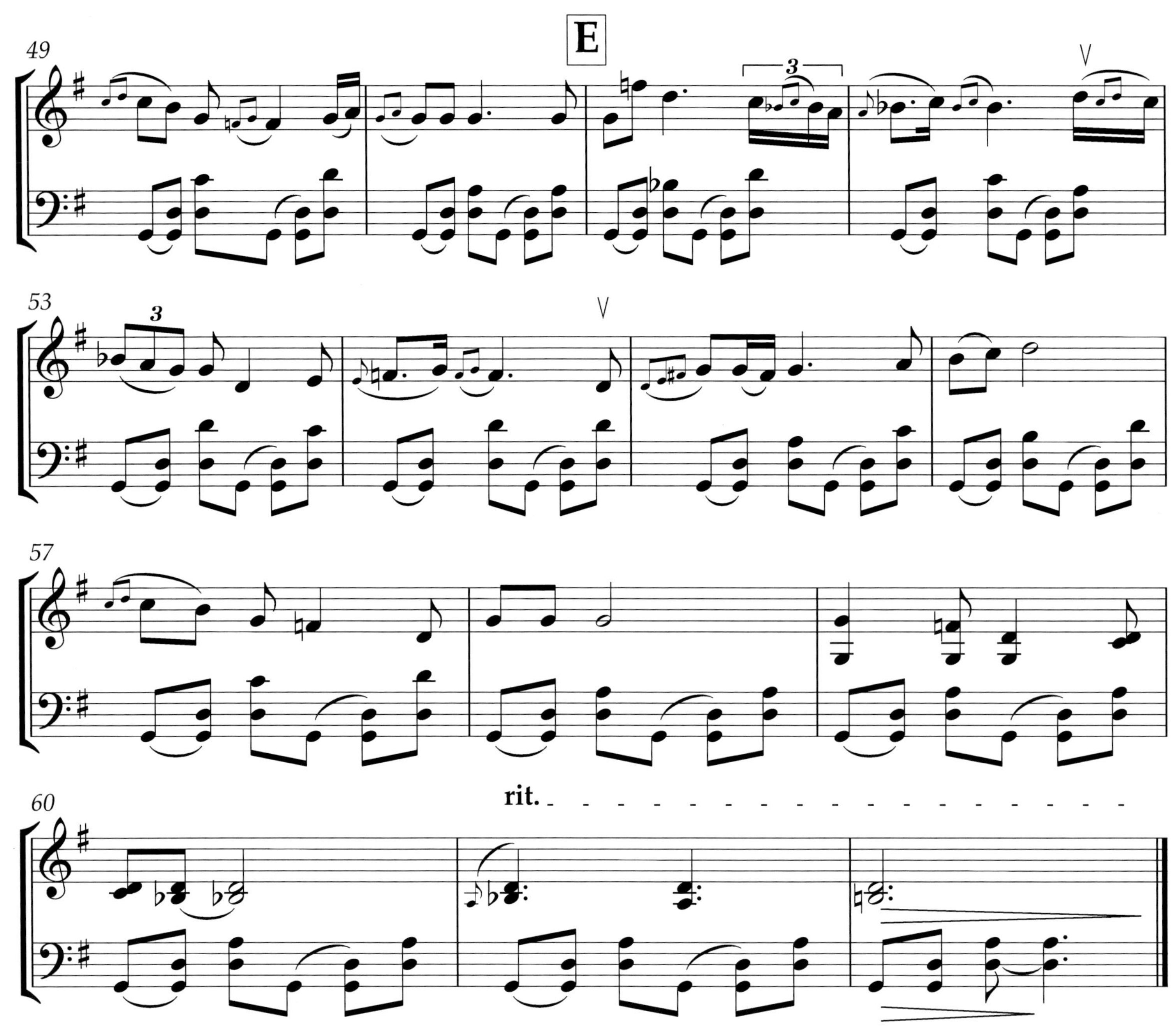
E
49
53
57
60
rit.

*This page has been left blank to avoid an awkward page turn.*

7

# Bring a Torch Jeannette, Isabella

Traditional French
Arranged by the Wires: Sascha Groschang and Laurel Parks

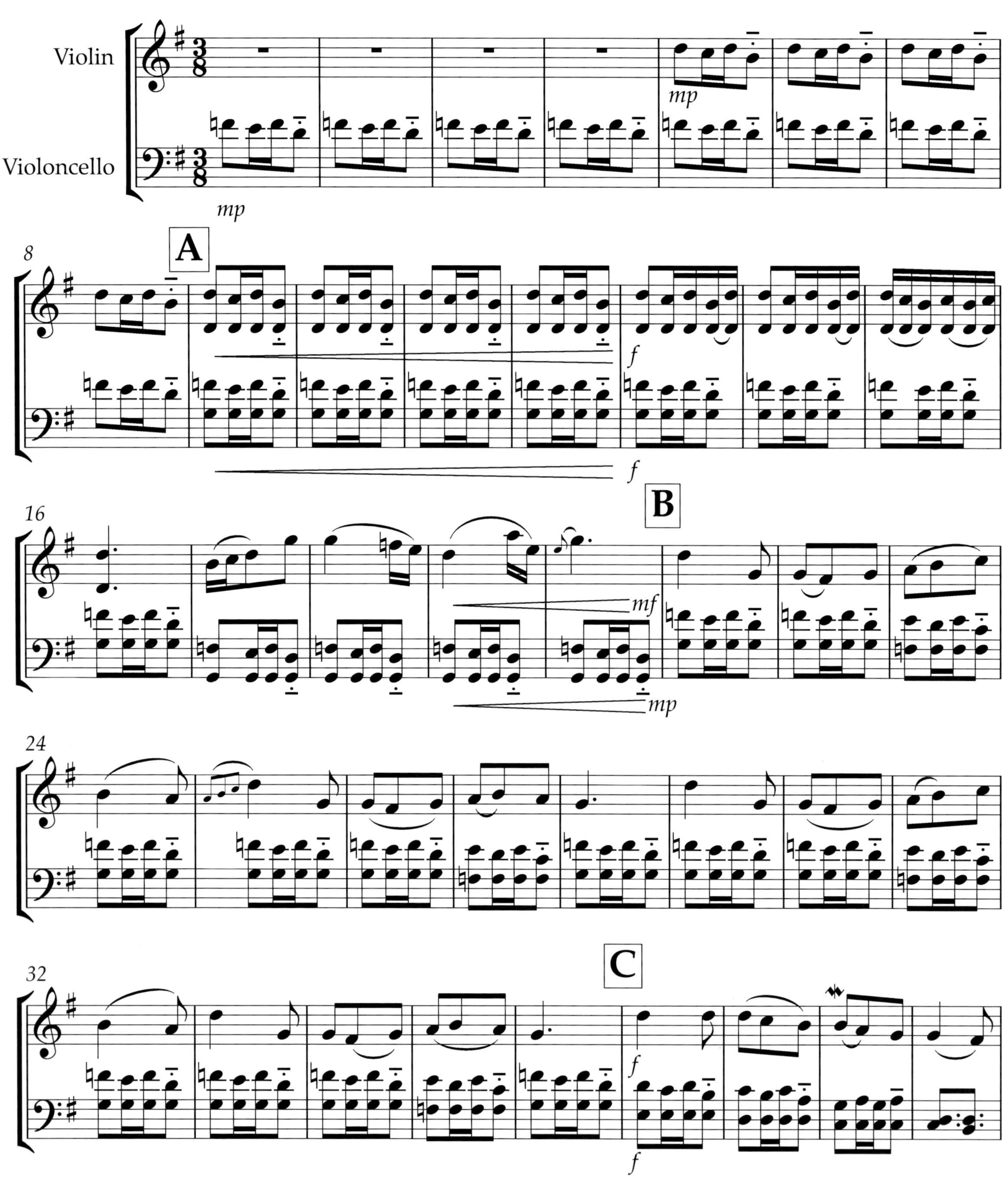

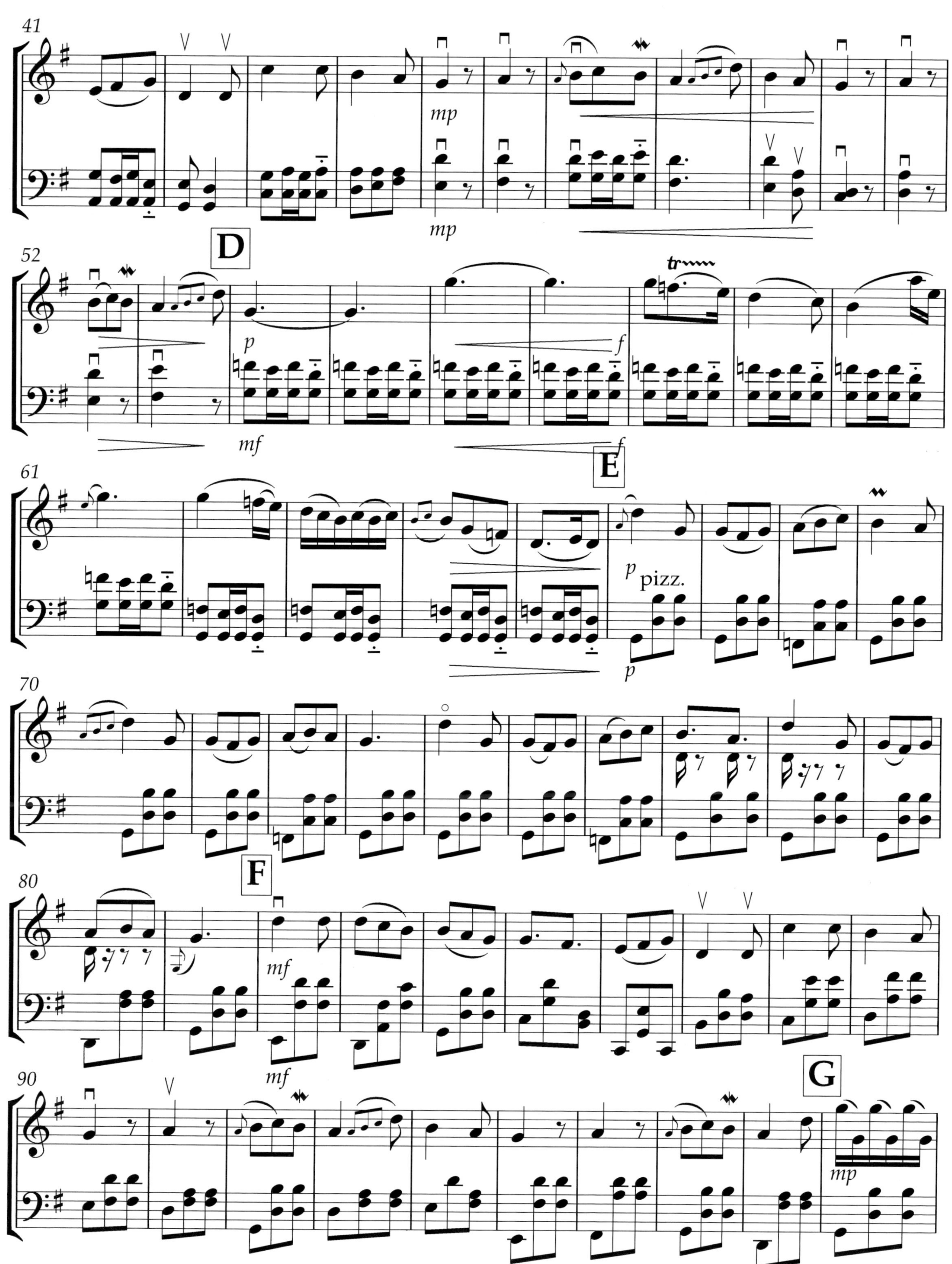
41
mp
mp
52
D
p
f
mf
f
61
E
p
pizz.
p
70
80
F
mf
mf
90
G
mp

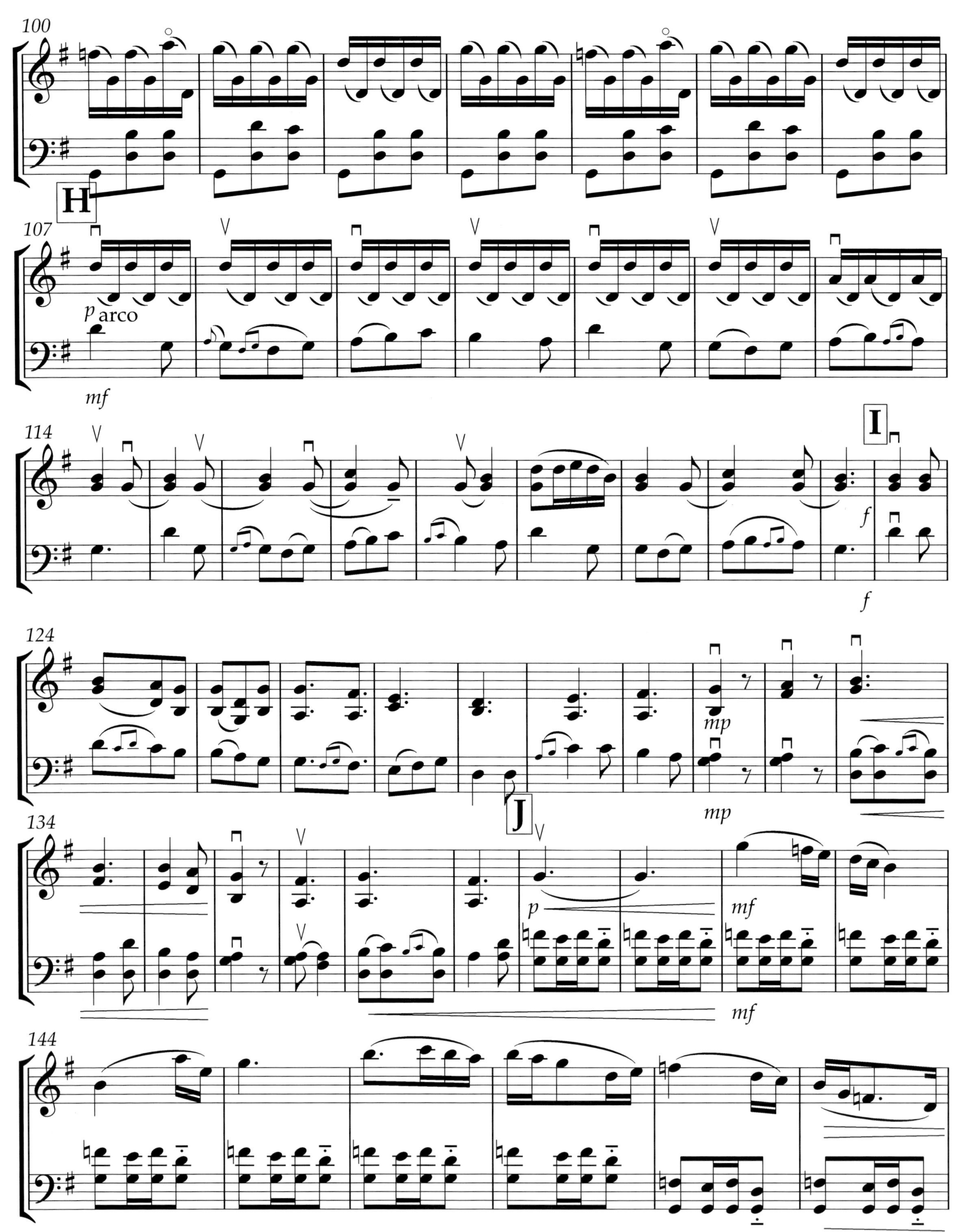
100
H
107
p arco
mf
114
I
f
f
124
mp
mp
134
J
p
mf
mf
144

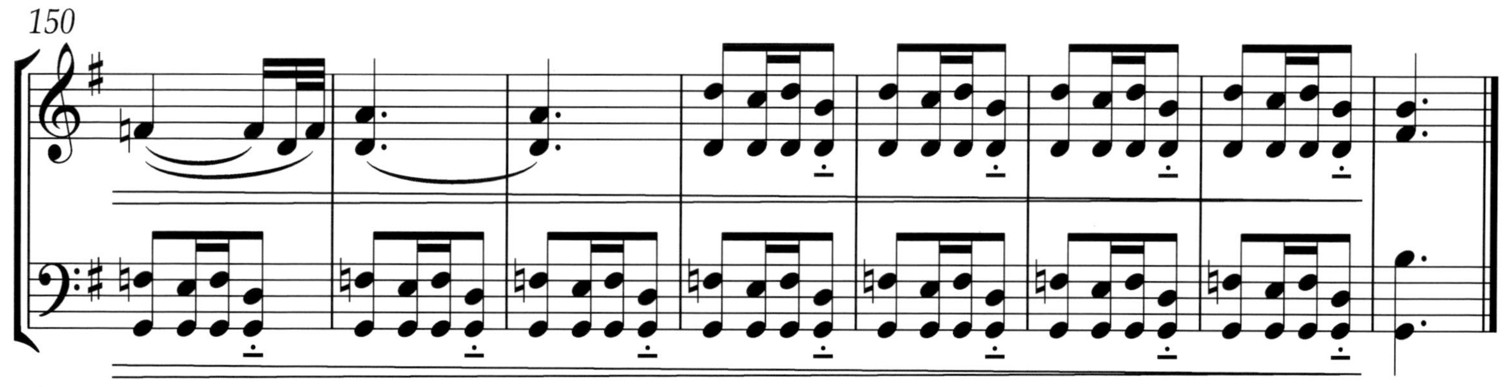
150

# In the Bleak Midwinter

Gustav Holst

Arranged by The Wires: Sascha Groschang and Laurel Parks

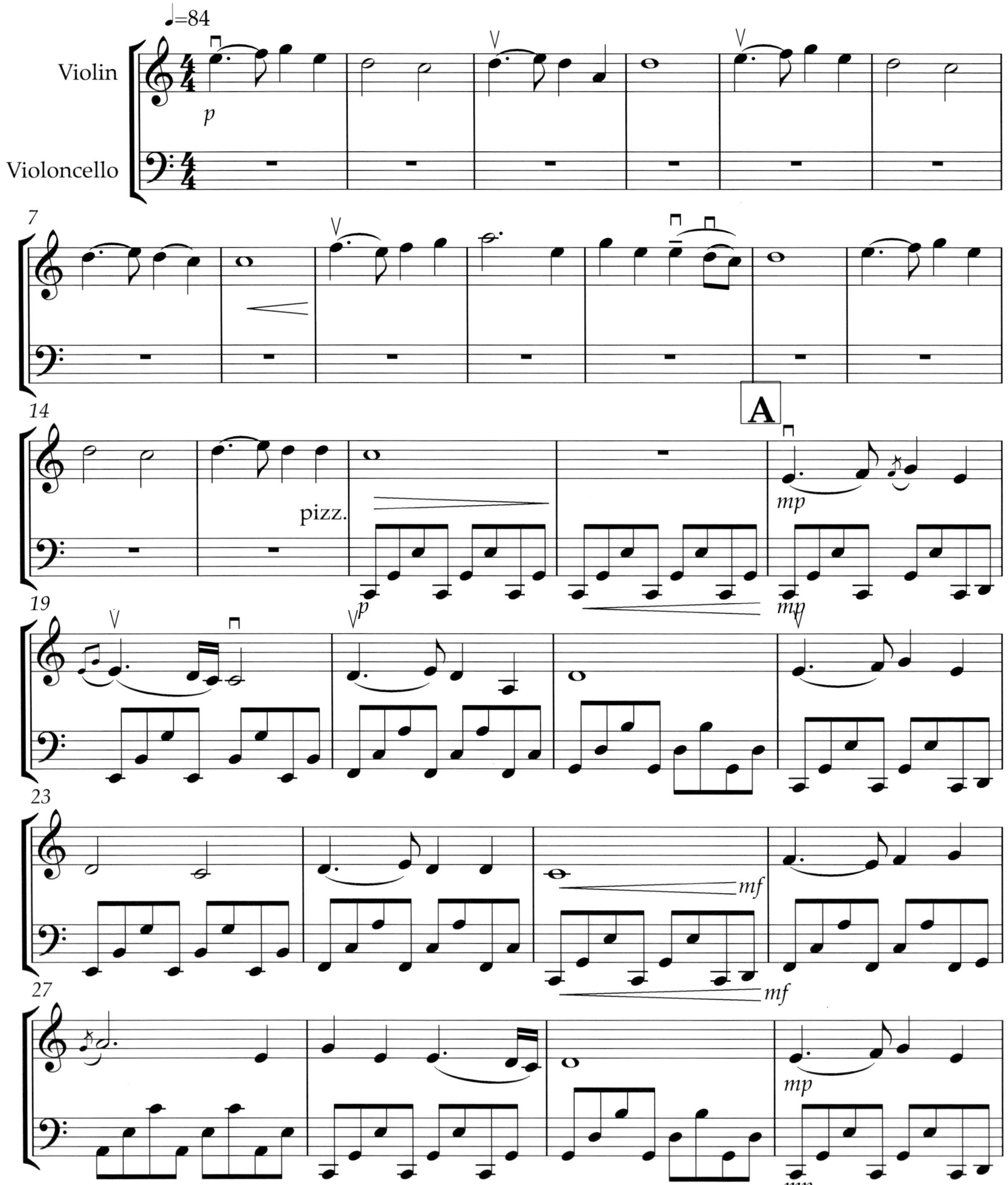

♩=84

Violin

Violoncello

*p*

7

14

pizz.

A

*mp*

19

*p*

*mp*

23

*mf*

27

*mp*

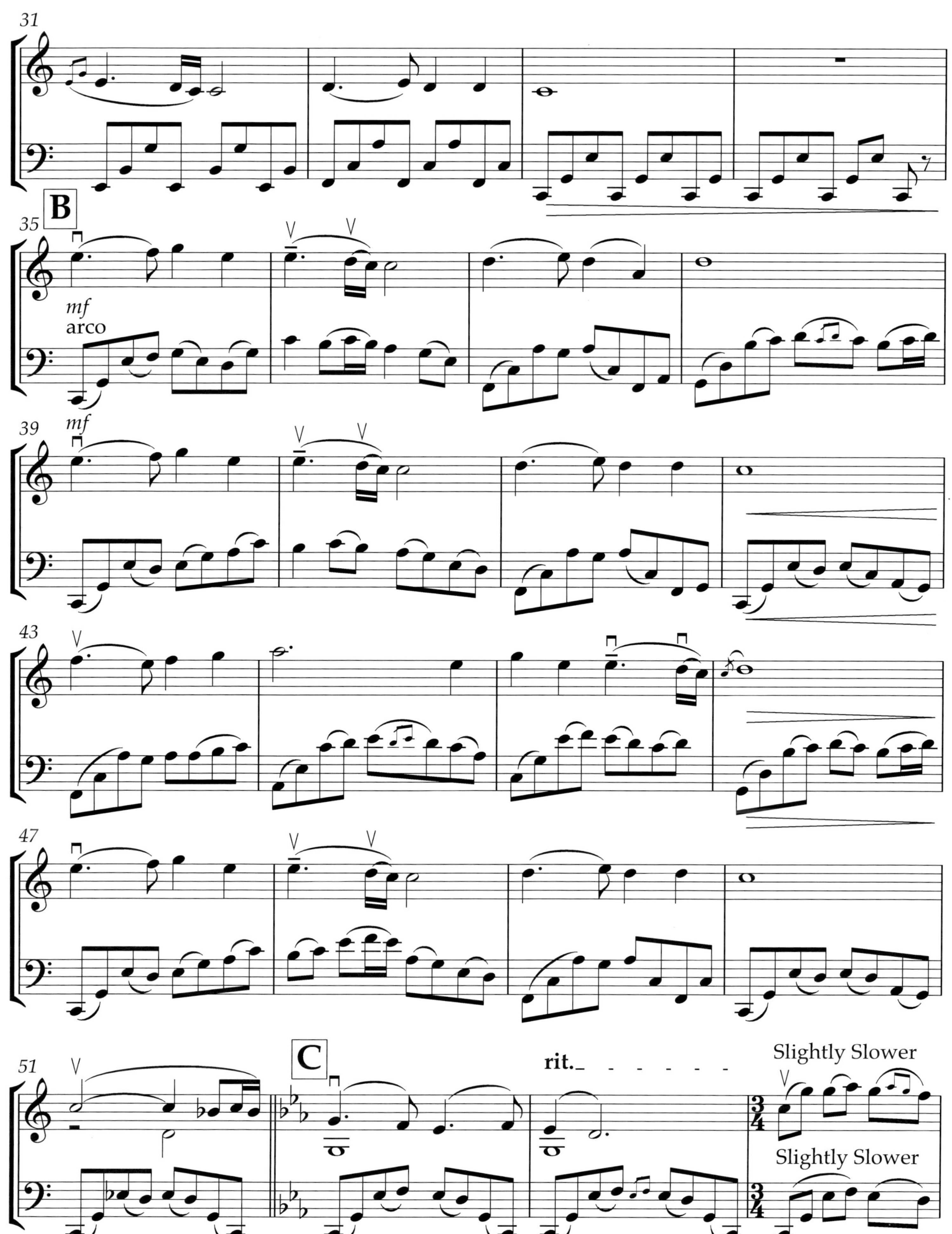
B
mf
arco
mf
C
rit.
Slightly Slower
Slightly Slower

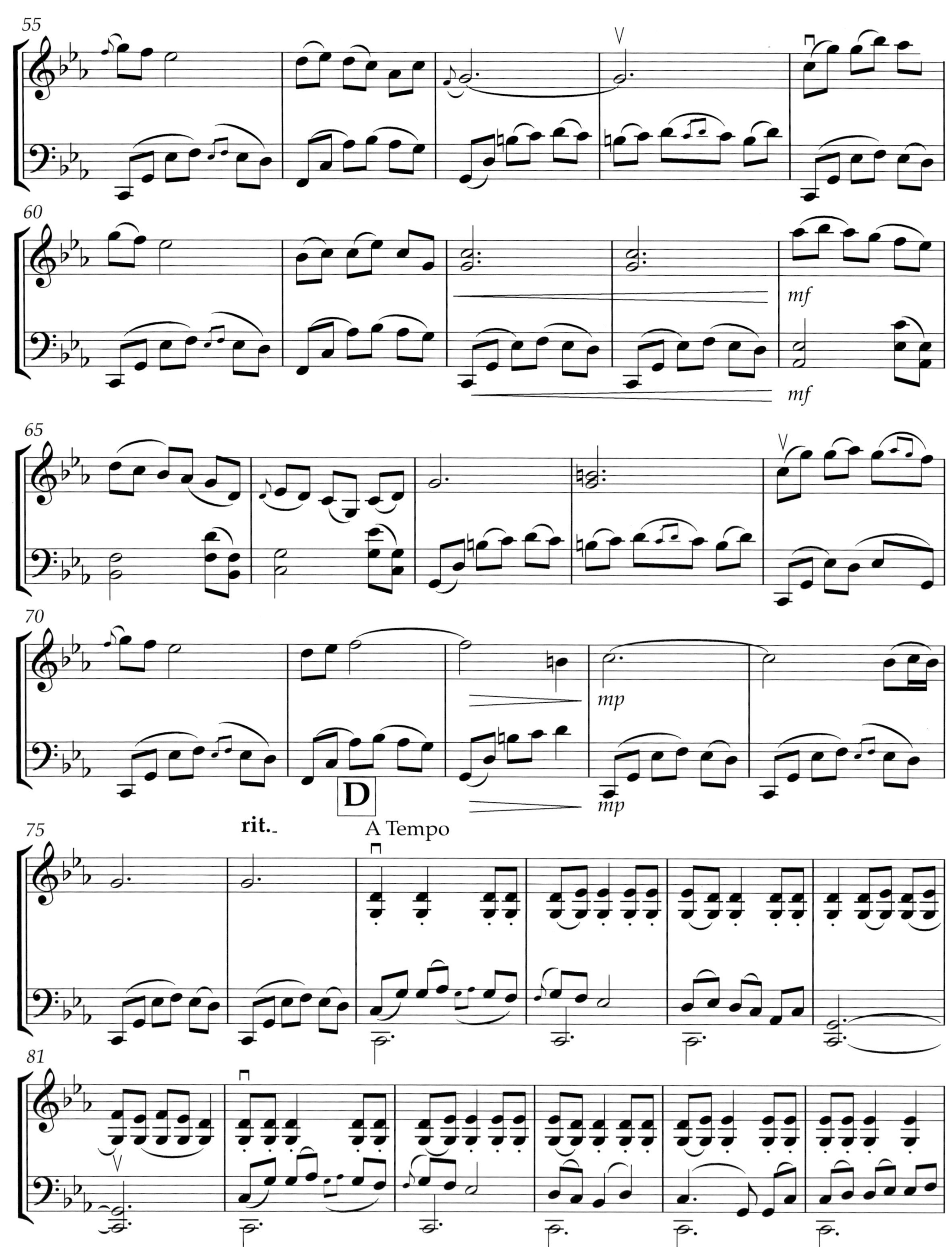

55
60
mf
mf
65
70
mp
D
mp
75
rit.
A Tempo
81

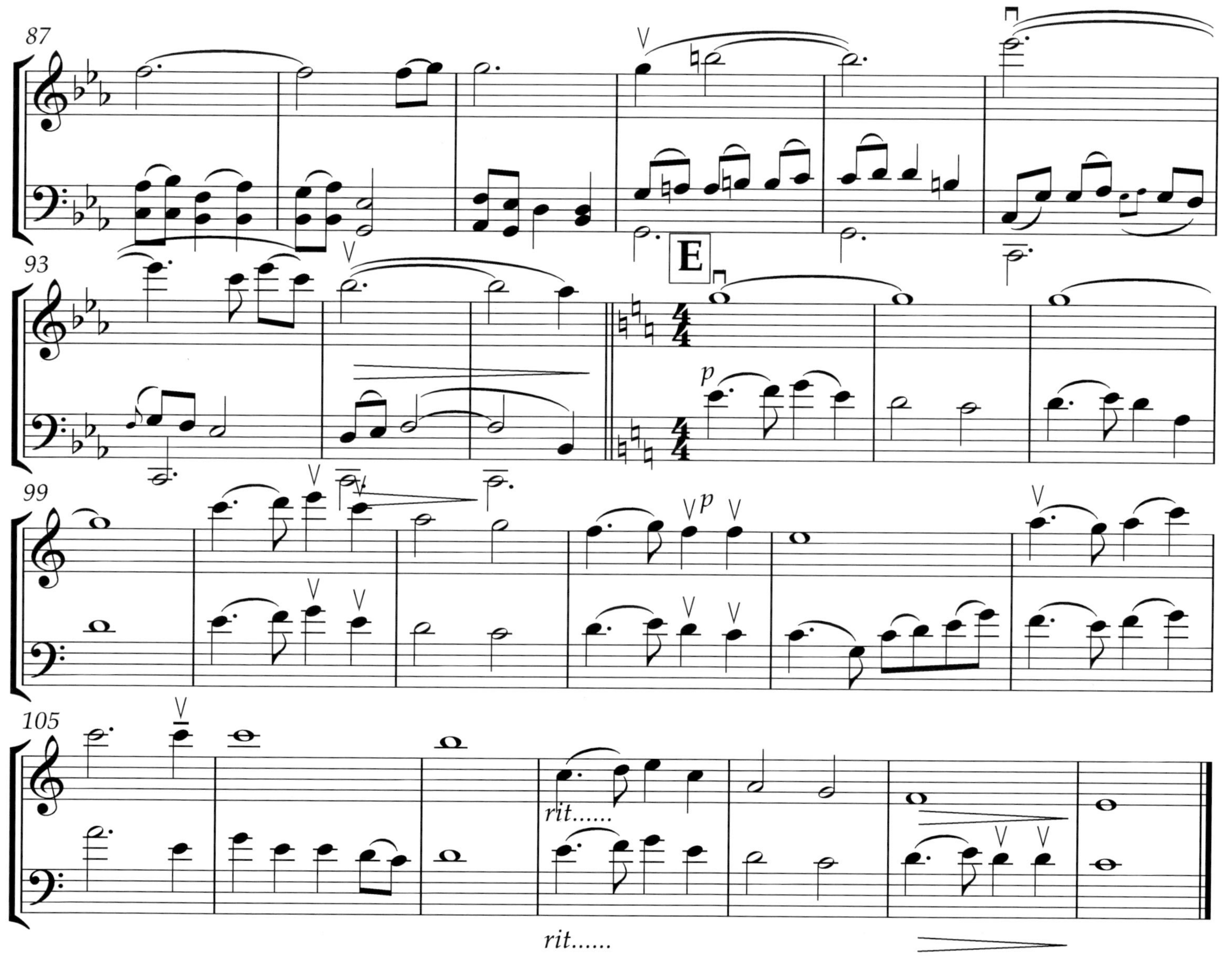
87
93
E
p
99
p
105
rit......
rit......

# Campbell Street

The Wires: Sascha Groschang and Laurel Parks

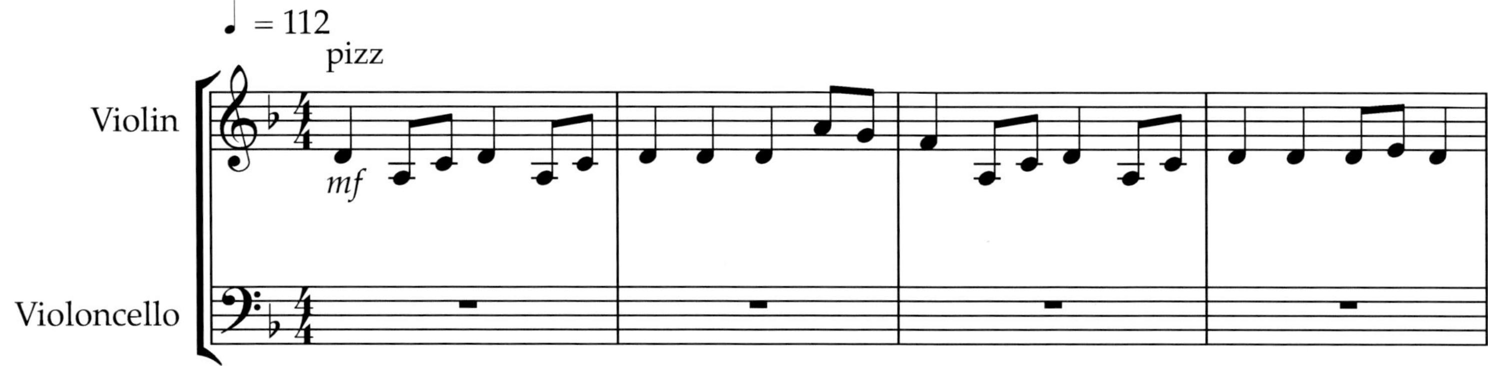


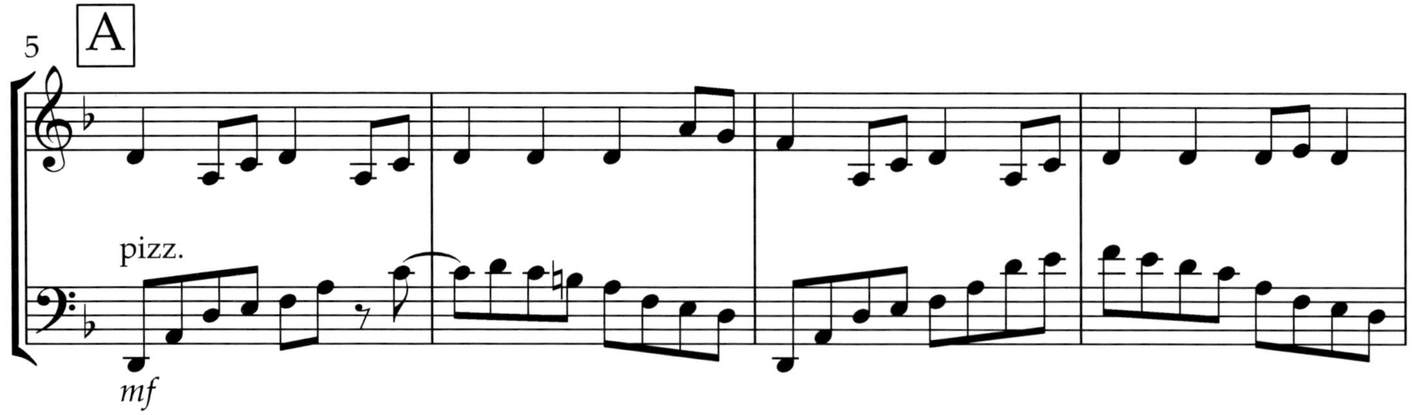


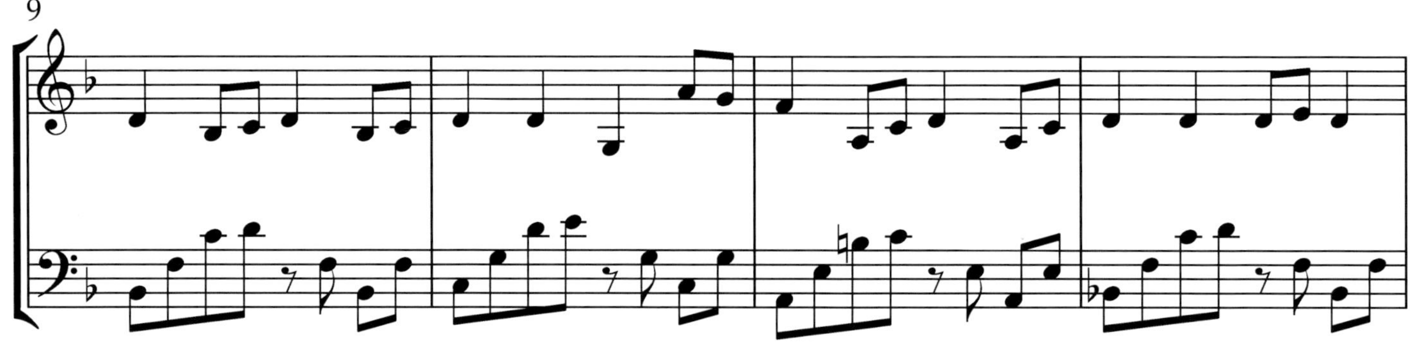


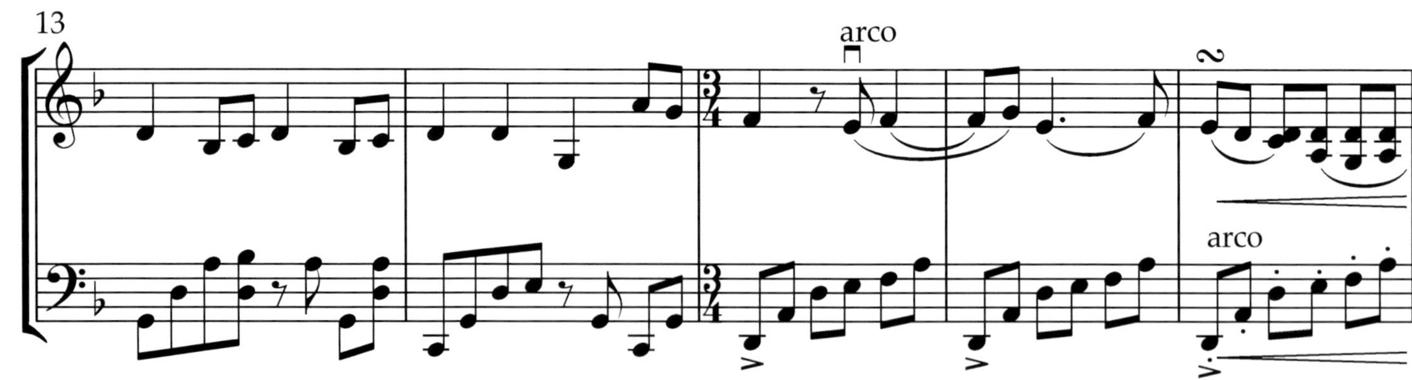

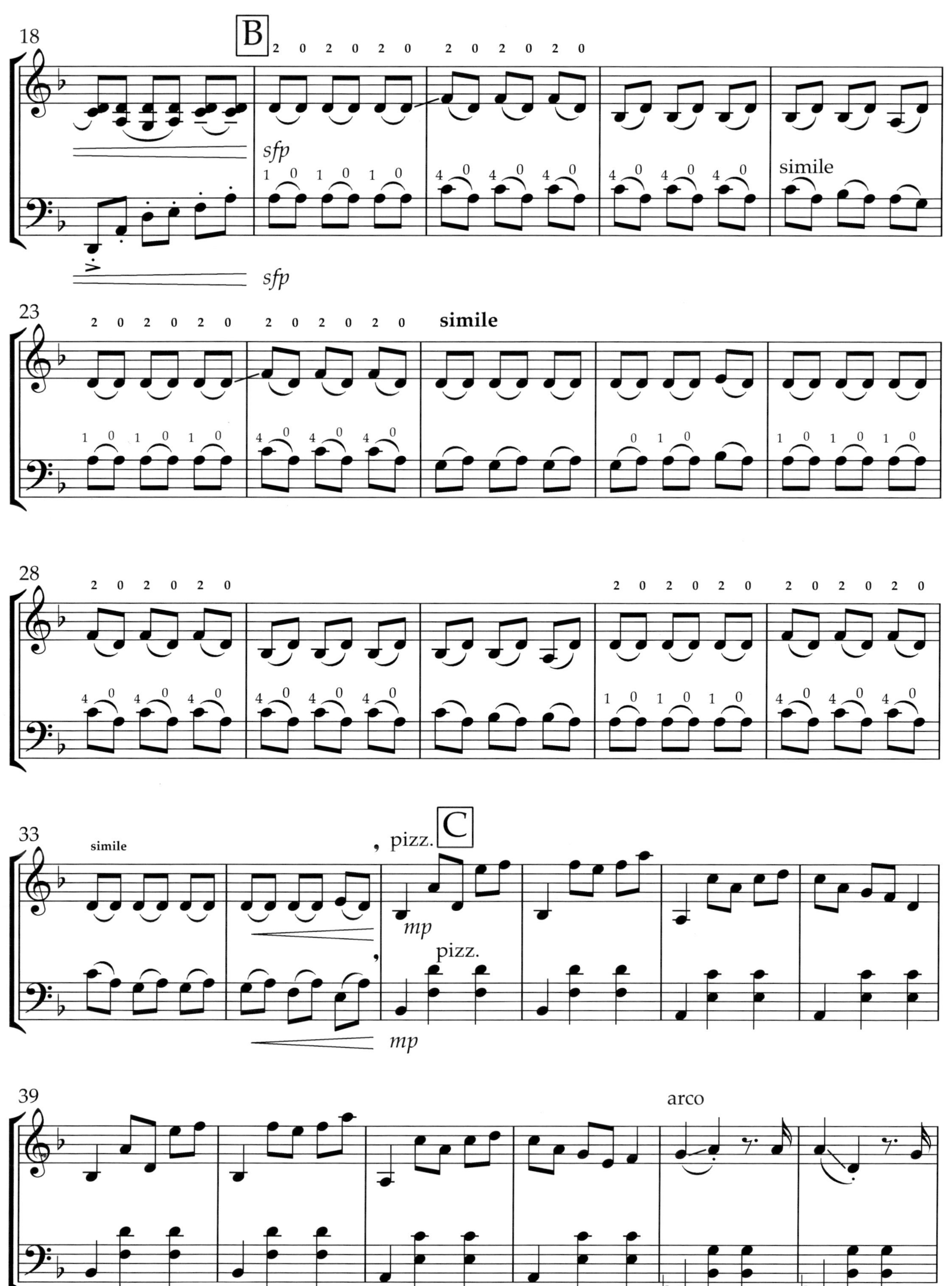
18
B
sfp
simile
sfp
23
simile
28
33
simile
pizz.
C
mp
pizz.
mp
39
arco

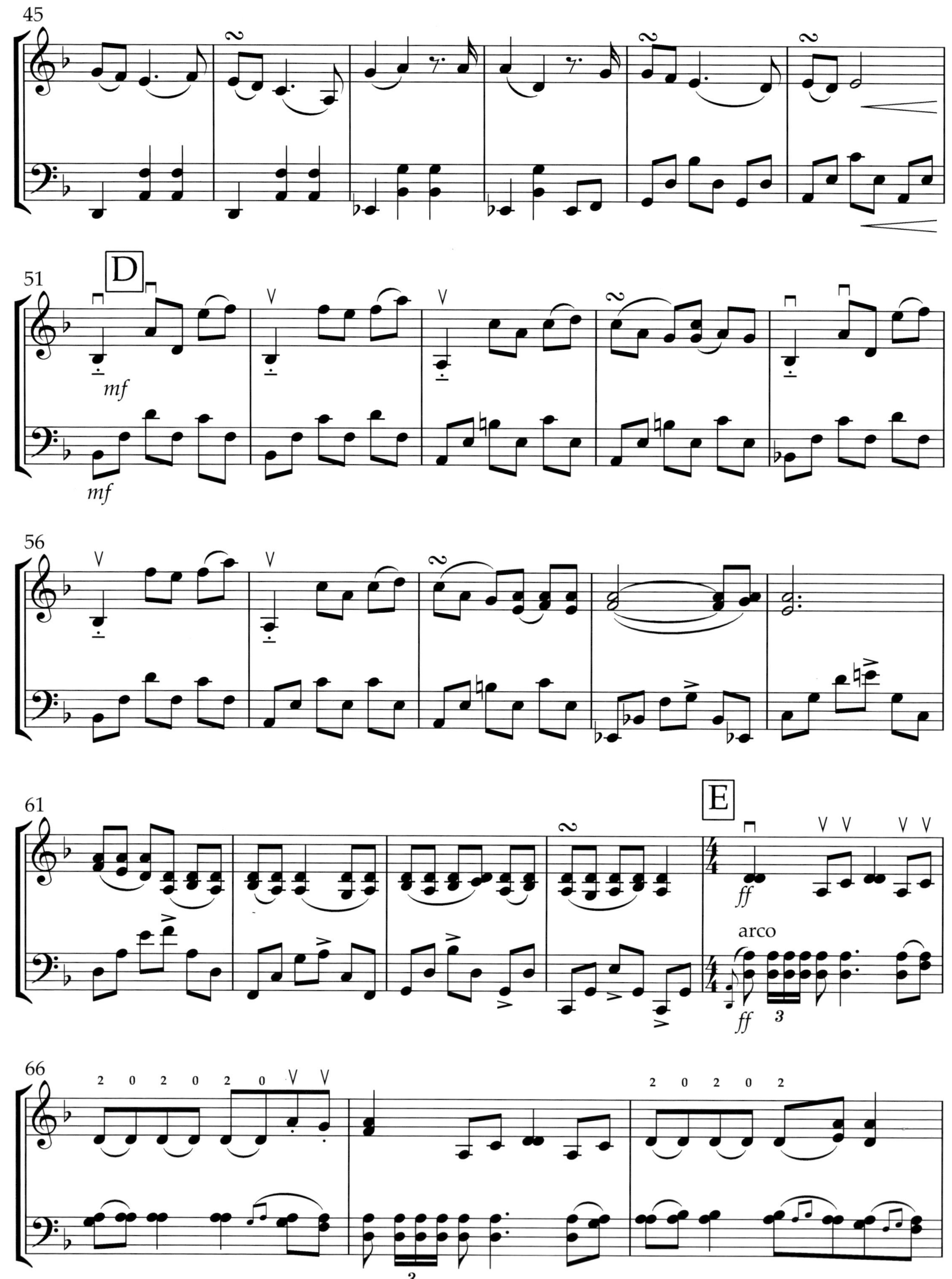
45
51
D
mf
mf
56
61
E
ff
arco
ff
3
66
2 0 2 0 2 0
3
2 0 2 0 2

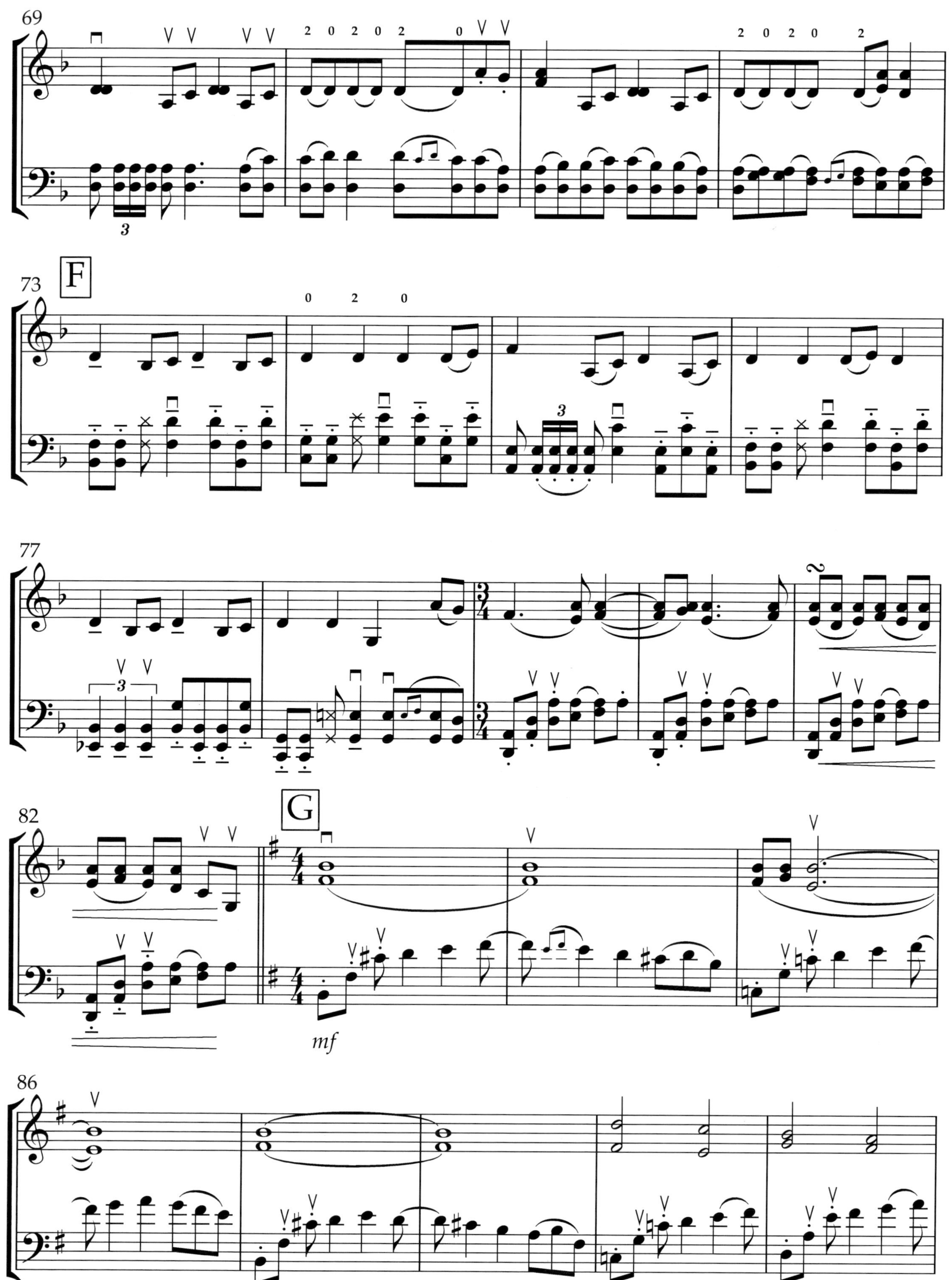
69
2 0 2 0 2 0
2 0 2 0 2
73
F
0 2 0
77
82
G
mf
86

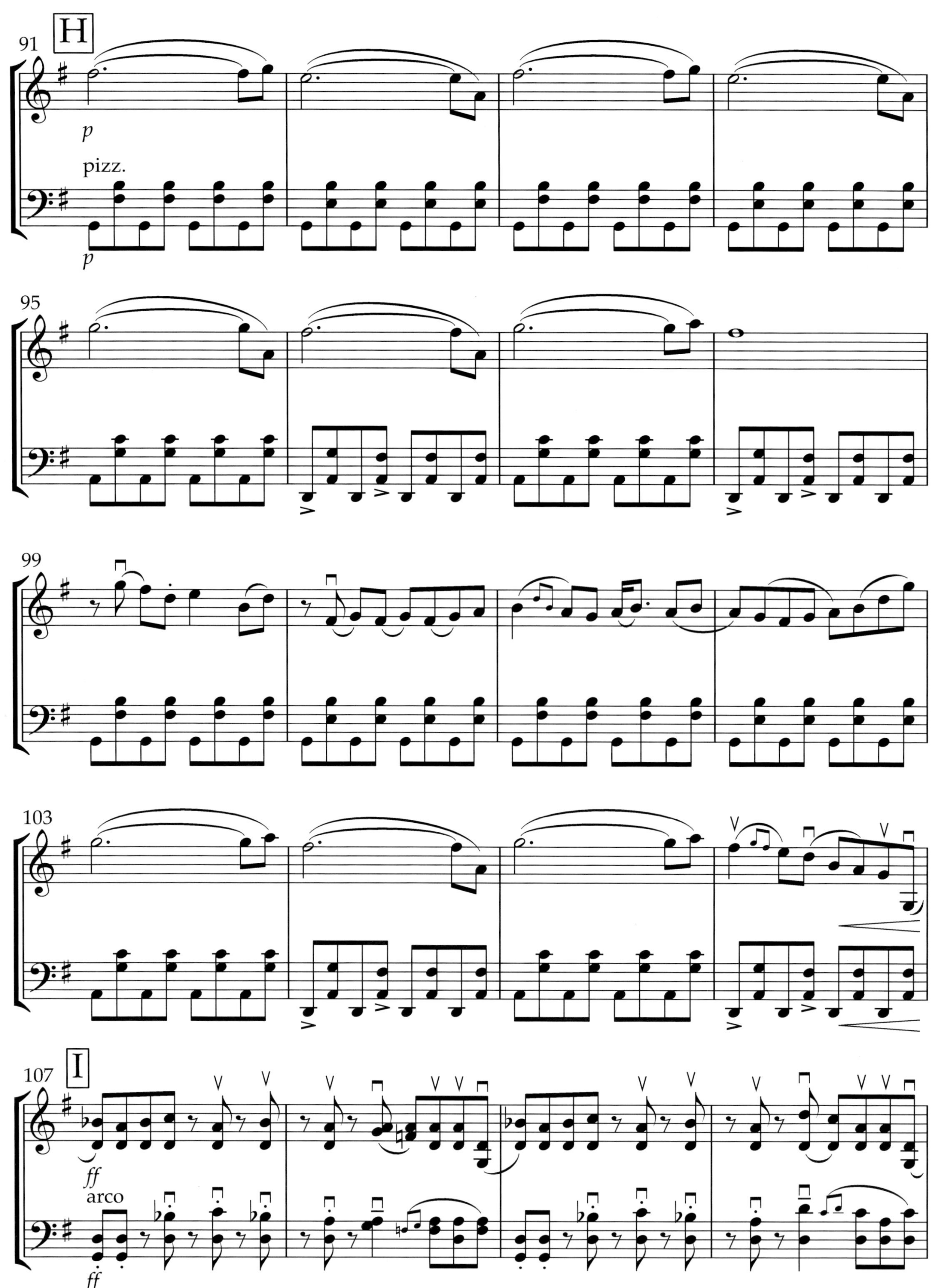
H
91
p
pizz.
p
95
99
103
107
I
ff
arco
ff

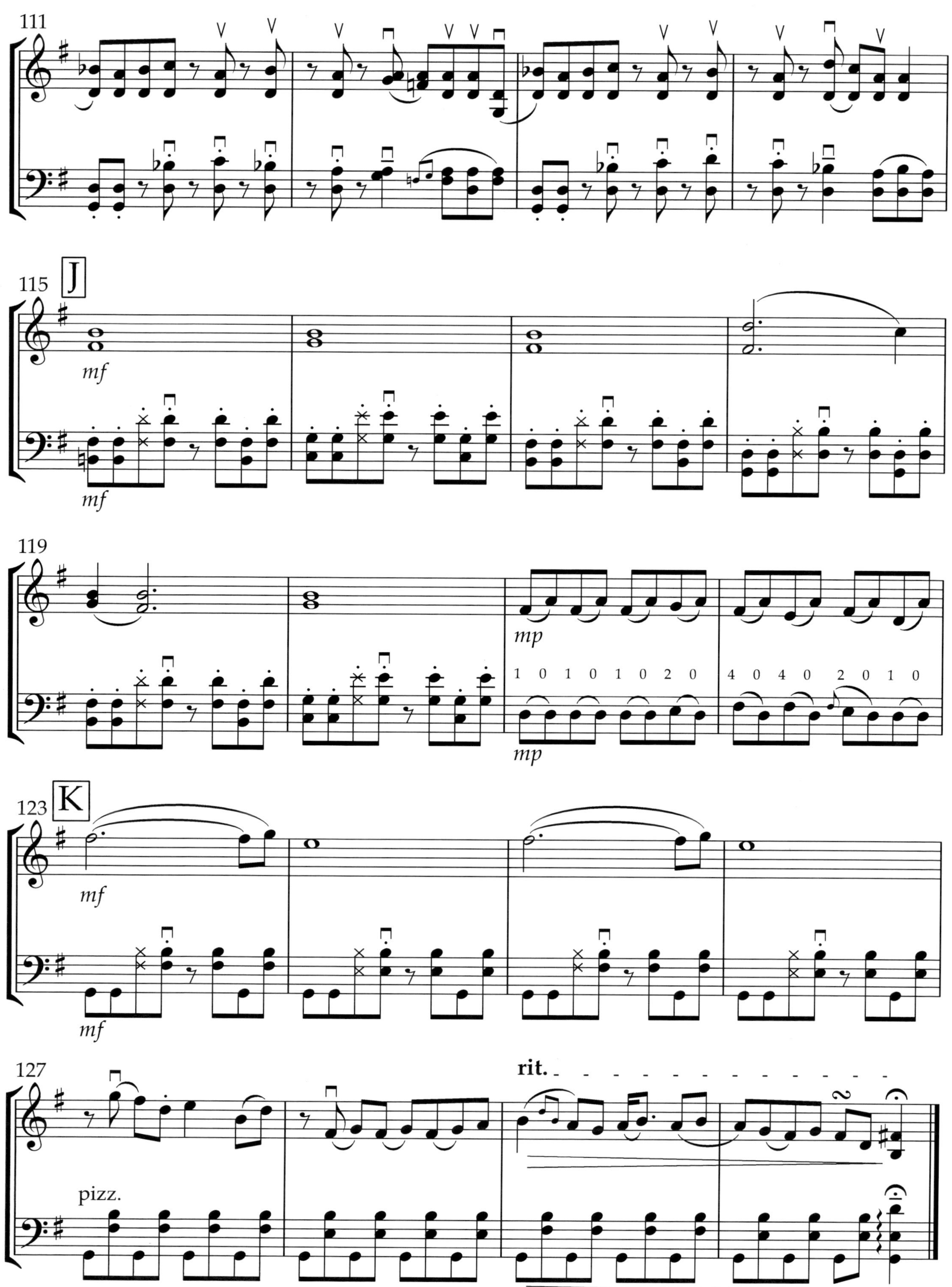
111
115
J
mf
mf
119
1 0 1 0 1 0 2 0
4 0 4 0 2 0 1 0
mp
mp
123
K
mf
mf
127
pizz.
rit.

# Once in Royal David's City

Cecil Francis Alexander and Henry John Gauntlett
Arranged by The Wires: Sascha Groschang and Laurel Parks

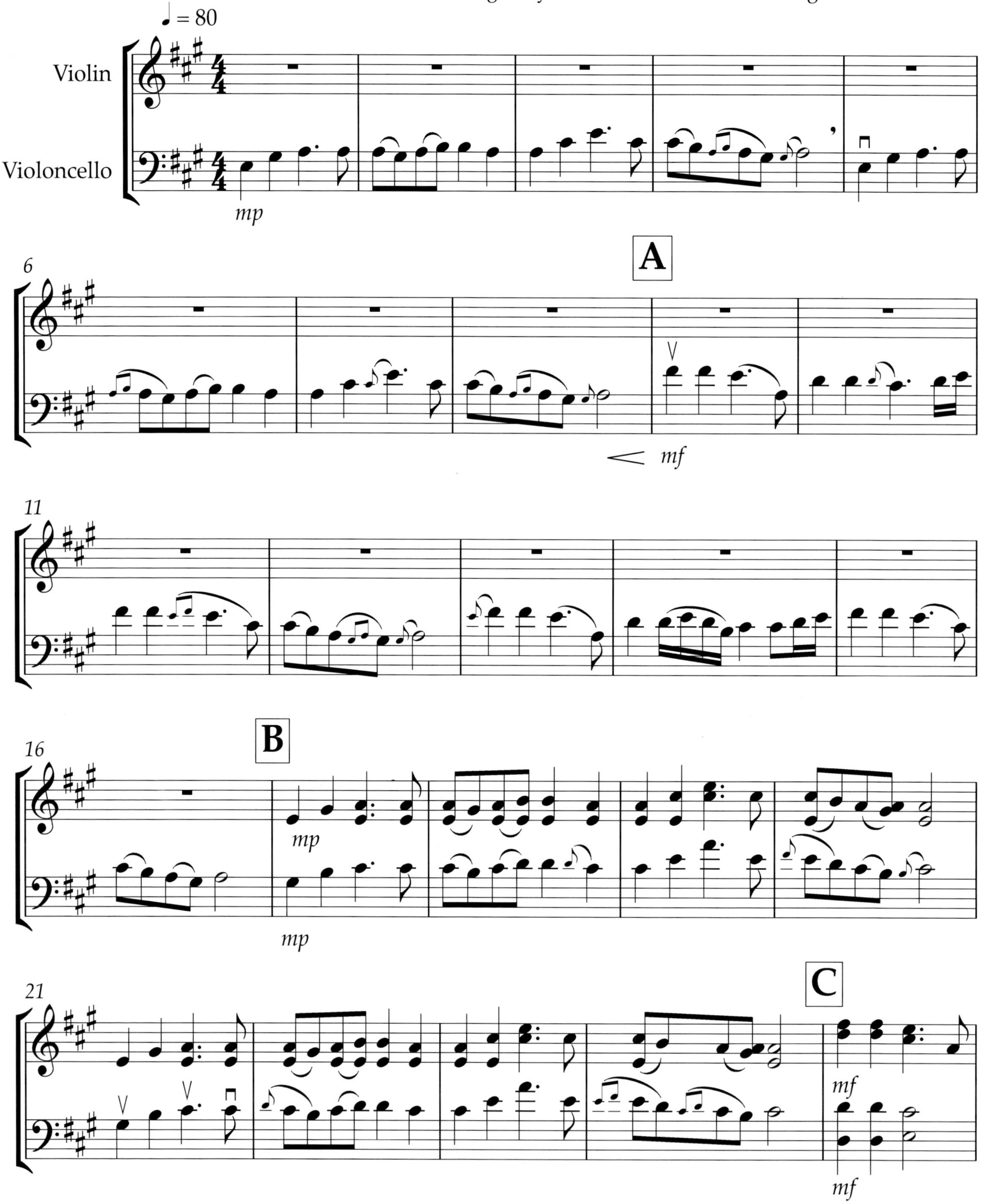

♩ = 80

Violin

Violoncello

*mp*

6

A

*mf*

11

16

B

*mp*

*mp*

21

C

*mf*

*mf*

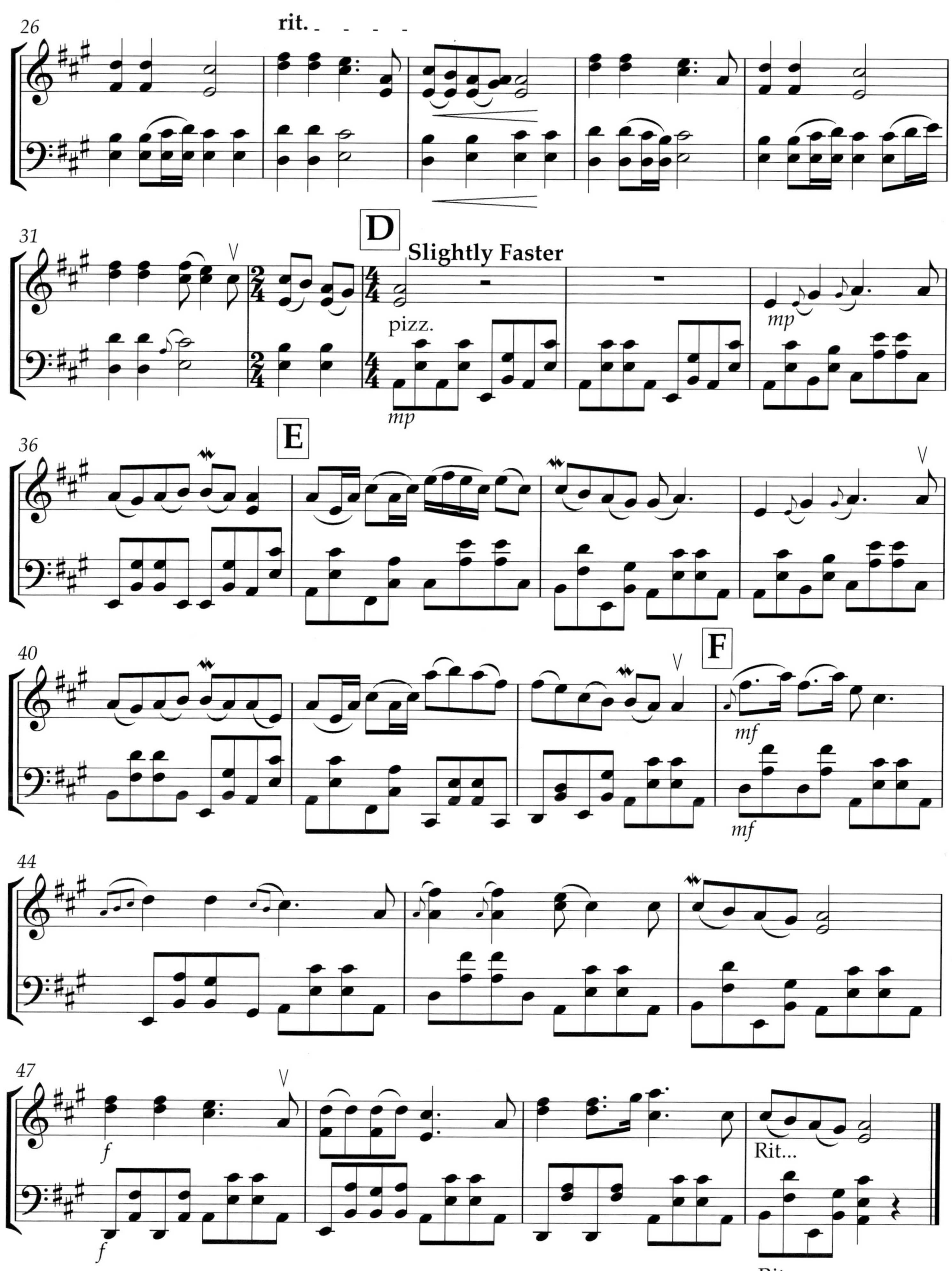
26
rit.
31
D
Slightly Faster
pizz.
mp
mp
36
E
40
F
mf
mf
44
47
f
f
Rit...
Rit...

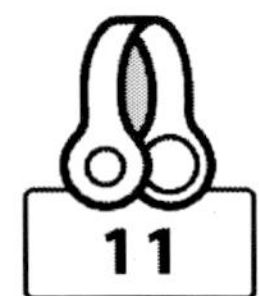


# *We Wish You a Merry Christmas*

Traditional English
Arranged by The Wires: Sascha Groschang and Laurel Parks

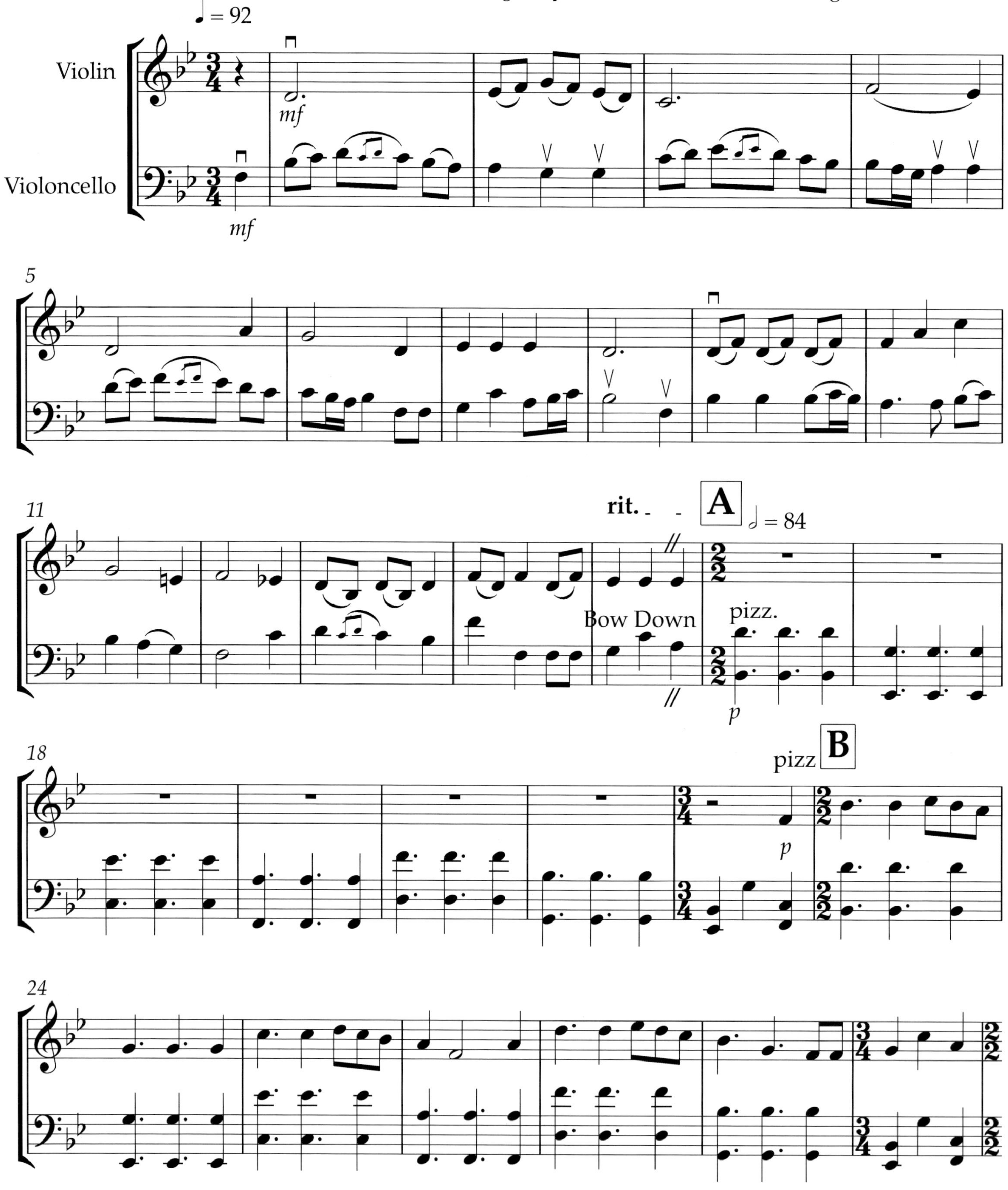

♩ = 92

Violin

Violoncello

*mf*

*mf*

5

11

rit.

**A**

𝅗𝅥 = 84

Bow Down

pizz.

*p*

18

pizz

**B**

*p*

24

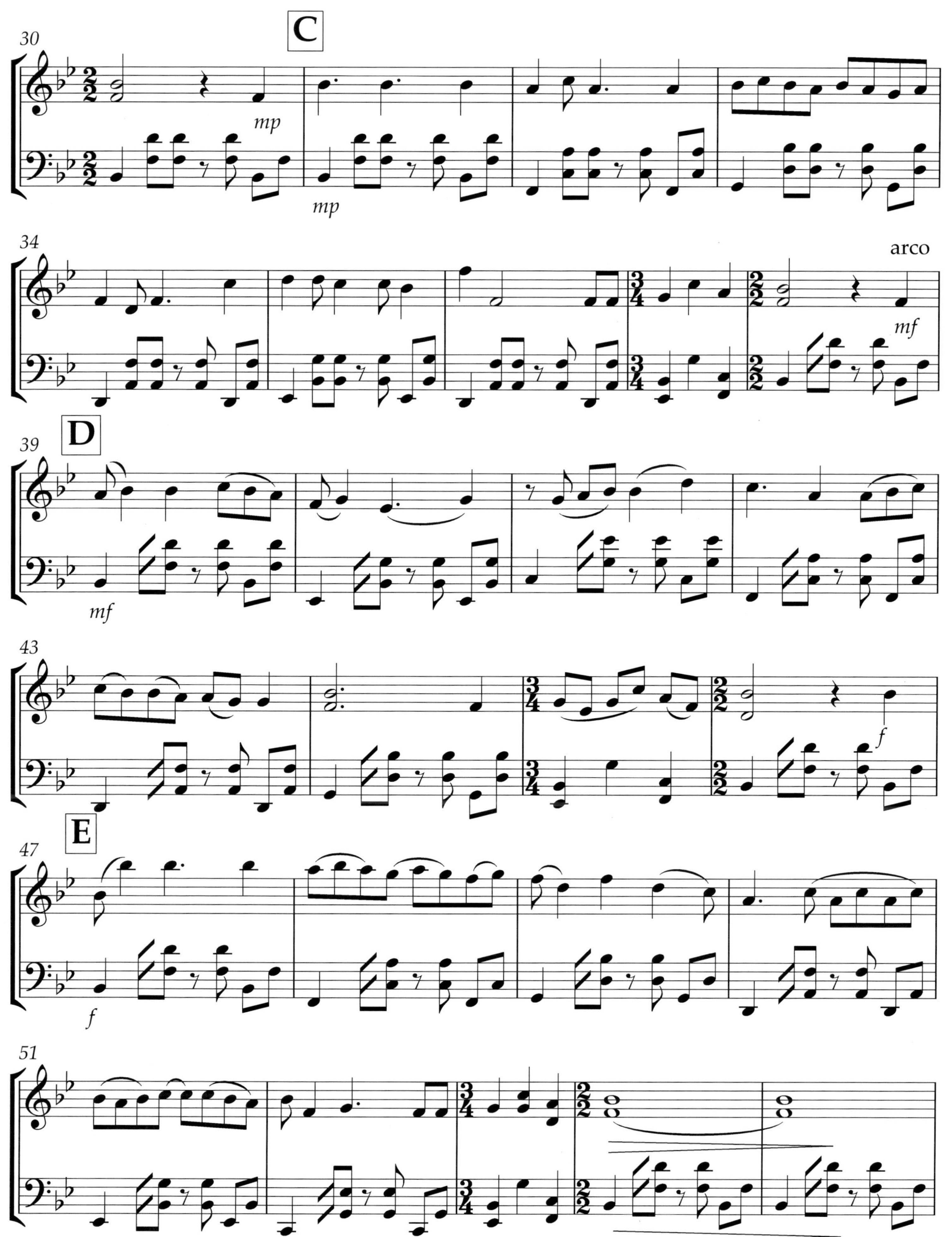
C
D
E
arco
mp
mp
mf
mf
f
f

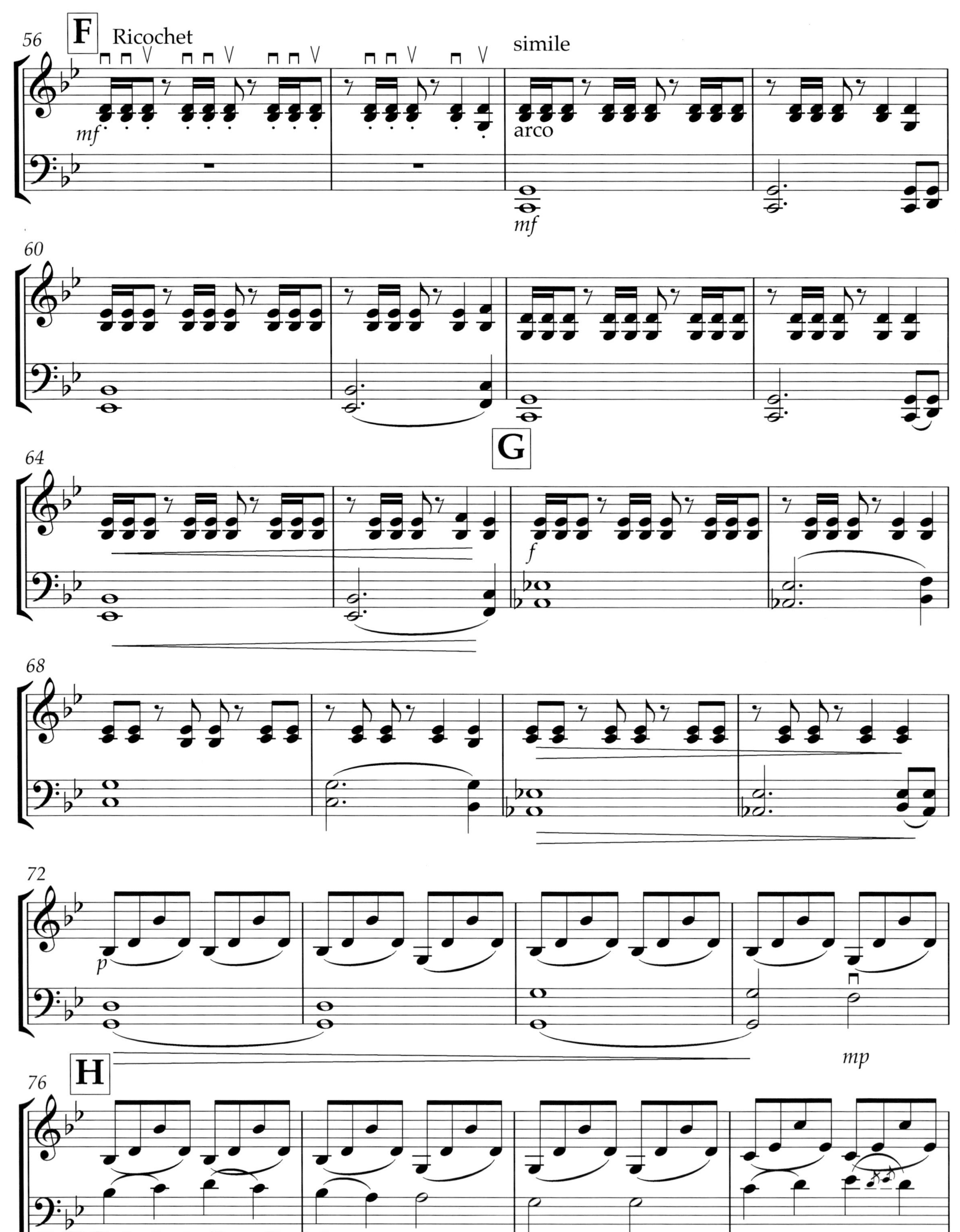
56
F
Ricochet
mf
simile
arco
mf
60
64
G
f
68
72
p
mp
76
H

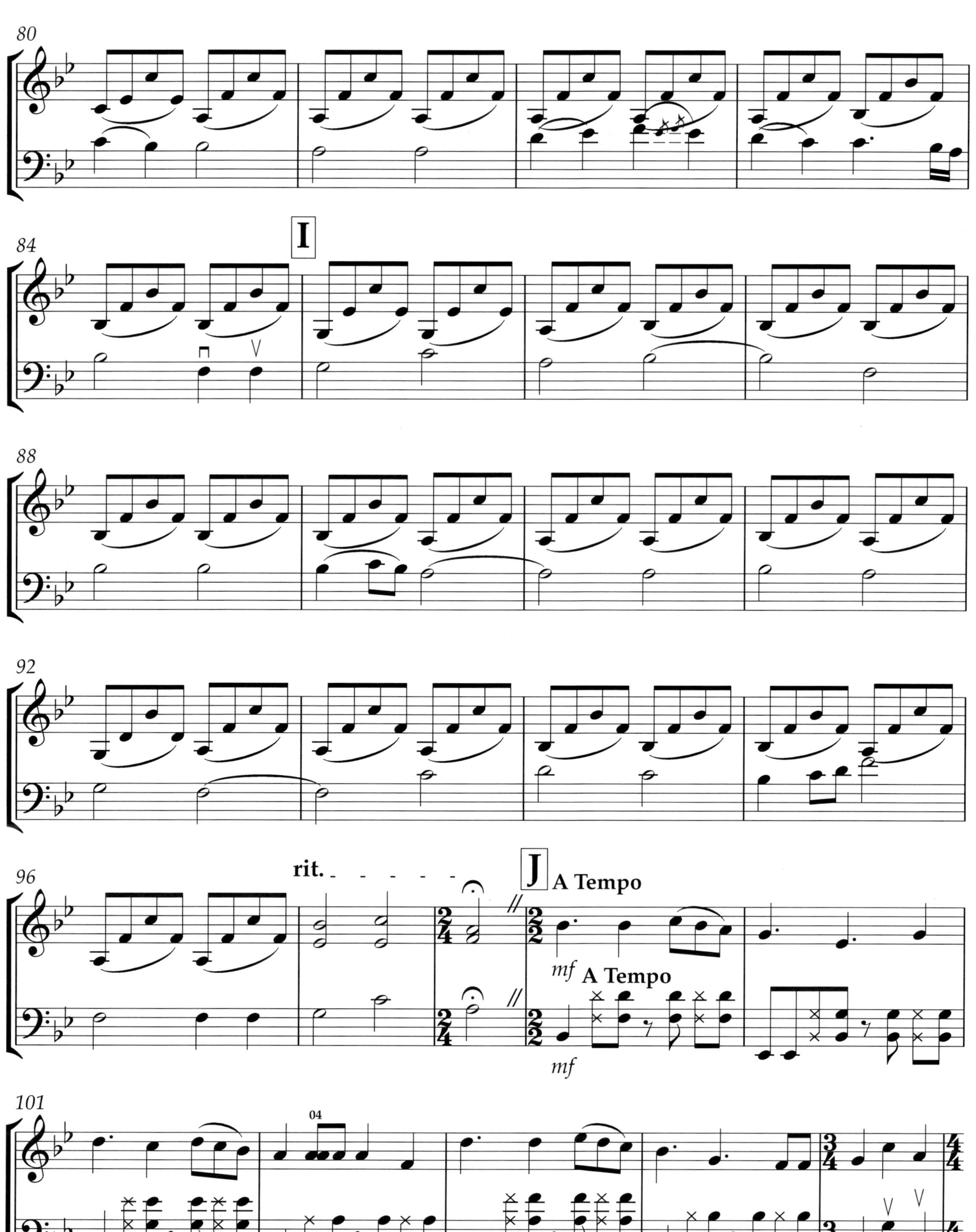
80
84
I
88
92
96
rit.
J
A Tempo
mf
A Tempo
mf
101
04

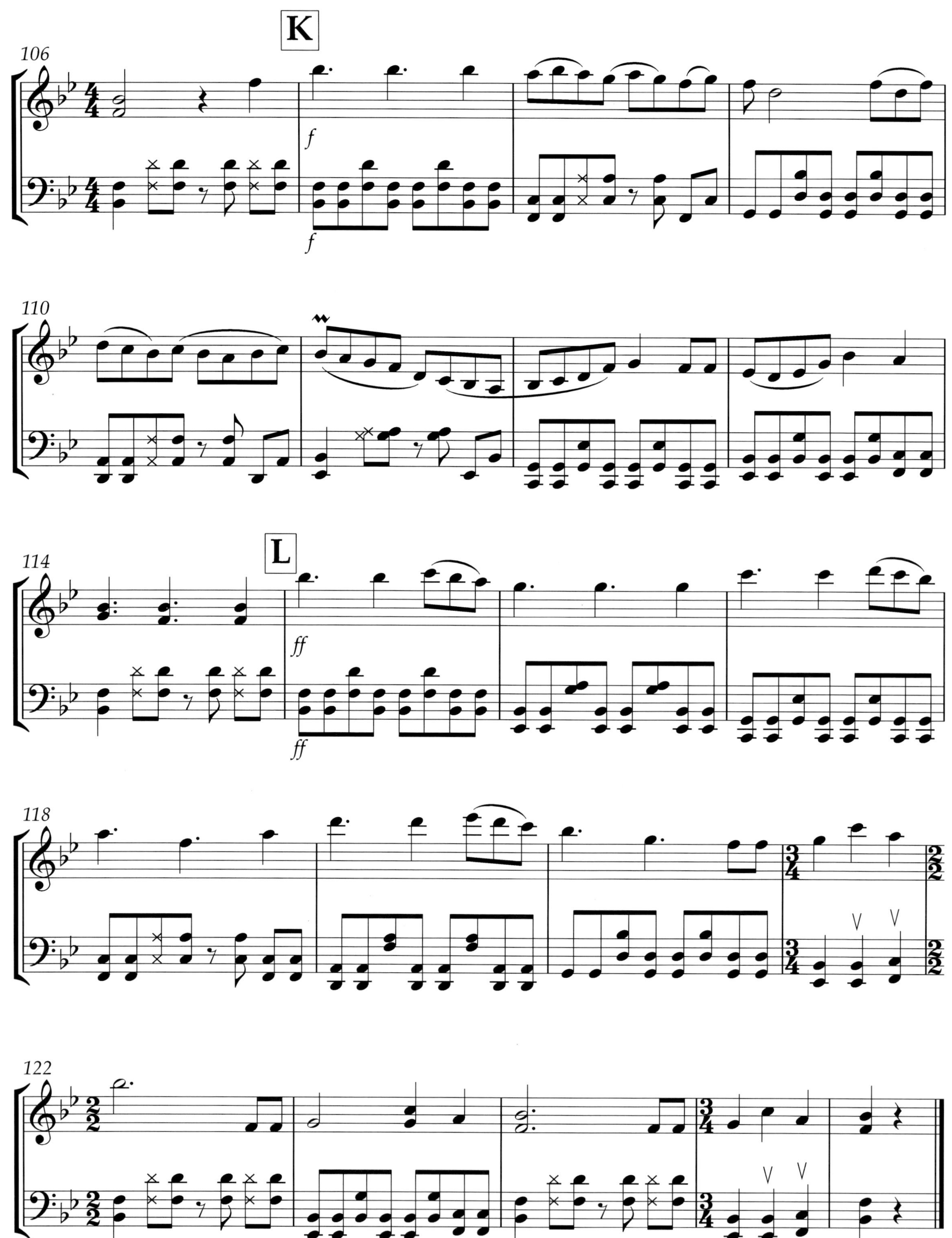
K
106
f
f
110
114
L
ff
ff
118
122

# *The Wires Duo*

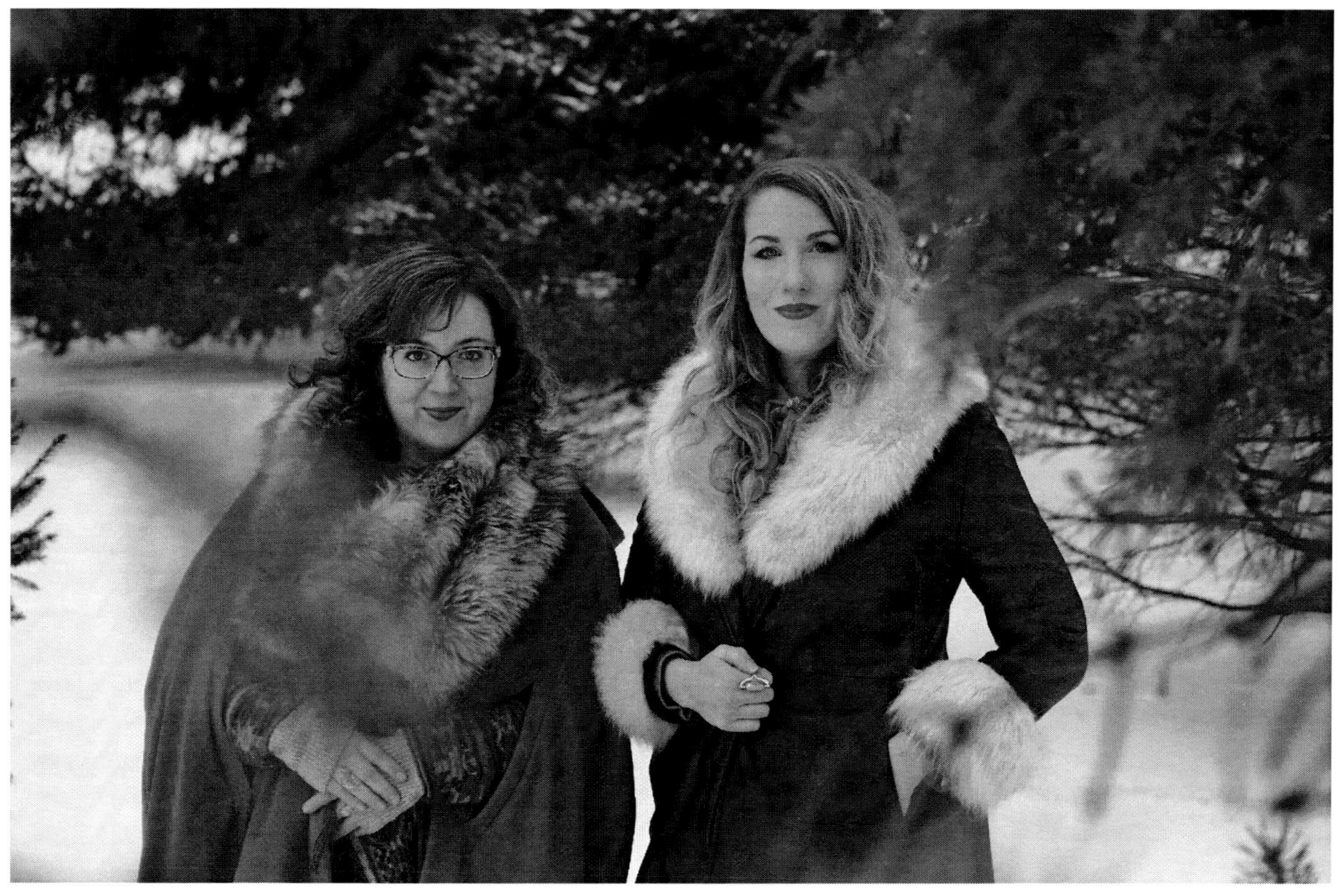

*Sascha Groschang, Cello* *Laurel Morgan Parks, Violin*

The Wires are a modern exploration in string sound. Created in Kansas City, Missouri, Laurel Morgan Parks, violin, and Sascha Groschang, cello, have been composing dynamic and cinematic music as best friends since 2009. Their music is inspired by imagery found in the natural world, folk styles, and modern string techniques. Following their debut album in 2012, their album "Wilder" (May 2019) is an imagined journey that includes depths of the oceanic world, the vast expanse of Celtic hills, the coldness of the frozen tundra and a discovery of the cosmos. Their holiday album, "Winter" (December 2020) encompasses cinematic, yet an intimate timbre, with the classic sounds of the season. The duo performs at festivals, concert halls, and music venues in the Midwest and beyond. Their online school, "Fiddle Life," (www. fiddlelife.com), teaches adults traditional styles at beginner and intermediate levels.

# *Other Mel Bay Violin Books*

American Fiddle Tunes for Solo and Ensemble: Violin 1 and 2 (C. Duncan)
Beautiful Melodies from Around the World - Music for Two Violins (Cooper)
Celtic Fiddle Tunes for Solo and Ensemble: Violin 1 and 2 (C. Duncan)
Christmas Music Arranged for Violin Duet (Staidle)
Christmas Strings: Violin 1 & 2 with Piano Accompaniment (Miller)
Come Fiddle with Me, Violin Duets (Hay)
Come Fiddle with Me, Violin Duets Volume Two (Hay)
Eastern European Music for Violin Duet (Harbar)
Easy Duets for Violin (Puscoiu)
Easy Violin Duets in First Position (Isaac)
Fiddling Classics for Solo and Ensemble: Violins 1 and 2 (C. Duncan)
First Lessons Violin Duets (C. Duncan)
J. S. Bach: Duets for Two Violins (Spencer/Engle)
Jazz Duets: Violin Edition (Biondi)
Music from Around the World for Solo and Ensemble: Violin 1 & 2 (Miller)
Ragtimes for 2 Violins (Brydern)
Scottish Airs and Dances for Violin Solo or Duet (Witt)
Scottish Melodies for Violin Solo or Duet (Witt)
Twin Fiddling (Phillips)
Violin Duet Classics Made Playable (Harbar)
Wedding Music for String Quartet (Staidle)
Wedding Music for Two Violins (Staidle)
100 Christmas Carols and Hymns for Violin and Guitar (C. Duncan)
100 Gospel Songs and Hymns for Violin and Guitar (C. Duncan)
100 Hymns for Violin and Guitar (W. Bay/C. Duncan)
Christmas Melodies for Violin Solo (C. Duncan)
Christmas Solos for Beginning Violin (C. Duncan)
Complete Book of Wedding Music for Flute or Violin (Mickelson)
Gospel Violin (Guest)
Hymn Favorites for Violin (Abell)
Hymn Tunes for Unaccompanied Violin (Carlson)
Hymns Made Easy for Violin (Clarke)
Old English Hymns for Violin Solo (Cummings)
Sacred Hymns for Violin (Isaac)
Sacred Violin Solos (Isaac)
Sacred Melodies for Violin Solo (C. Duncan)
Violin Solos on Early American Hymns Tunes (C. Duncan)
Wedding Music for Solo Violin (Curatolo)

# *Other Mel Bay Cello Books*

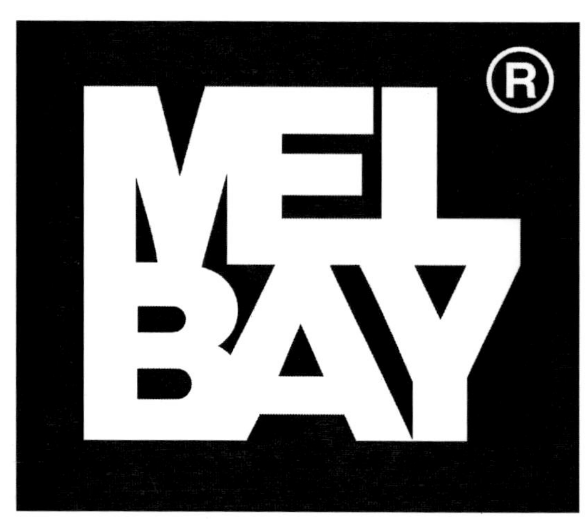
MEL
BAY